The Creative Writer's AI

Exploring ChatGPT as a Toolbox

Susan L Urban

JŪGUM PRESS

Published by Jūgum Press
Seattle, Washington U.S.A.
www.jugumpress.net

CONTENTS

The Creative Writer's AI

INTRODUCTION

> **Human:** what one word most accurately describes what AI is to humans

> **GPT-4:** Tool

The AI Toolbox

Hype and fear abound in the discussions of the potential for AI to change everything: To make scientific breakthroughs; to replace lawyers, programmers, and writers of marketing blogs; to magically transfigure into a singular general intelligence bent on turning humans into pets.

Whatever AI may be or become, right now it is a tool with an evolving set of capabilities, some of which are pretty exciting.

This book *seeks* to help you explore the practical applications of AI as a creative writer's aid while avoiding common traps, time wasters, and existential night terrors.

The discussions will cover these basics:

- What GPT-4 is and what it isn't.
- Roles AI can play in your writing.
- Custom prompts to help you in your writing life.

- Tips for crafting your own AI prompts.
- Traps and hallucinations to watch out for.
- Exercises to aid your exploration.

Using ChatGPT is as easy as having a conversation, but getting something useful out of that conversation takes planning. Without clear instructions and defined limits, AI—like everything else on the internet—can turn precious writing time into mornings wasted on outrage and dead ends.

We'll explore using clear effective prompts to handle specific time-saving activities such as tracking tasks, finding resources, targeted editing, and getting your work out into the world, allowing you to focus on your creative expression.

This book is for you—whether you are a fiction or non-fiction writer, or other creative looking for administrative help.

Get ready for an AI-fueled adventure tailored just for you, whether you want inspirational craft exercises, effective editing strategies, a perfect neighborhood setting for your American-foodie-in-Rome thriller, or a personal tutor to explain the mechanics of black hole space travel.

What This Book Is ... and Is Not

This book aims to cut through the hype so that you gain an understanding of and practical experience with how these tools might be useful right now.

What This Book Is Not. This is not a book about technology. I am not an AI expert, lawyer, technology enthusiast, or ethicist.

It is not a guide to using AI to generate content. Nor is it a how-to guide for editing AI-generated content to evade the AI-generated content-sniffing tools that are proliferating in the market.

It is not a resource for generating novels or stories as a side hustle.

This is not about replacing human creativity or outsourcing meaning and joy.

I am just a writer like you, having fun exploring a new tool.

Use This Book as a Guide. Read straight through or jump to whatever section sparks your interest. Experiment. If something doesn't help, don't do it. If you find something better, fantastic.

Part One introduces GPT-4 as an AI toolkit and explores the basics for working with GPT as a tool. My only recommendation: Before you dig into specific tools, read Chapter Two, "Using AI," to understand the components of an effective AI prompt.

Part Two covers various tools that AI can provide in a writing practice. Each discussion of a tool or role includes:

- Sample conversations with GPT-4.
- Specific prompts you can use in your writing practice.
- Tips and Cautions.
- Exercises to help you become familiar with the limits and potential of your AI tools.

Part Three looks at ways to use AI to get your creative work out into the world.

The Appendix includes:

- A quick sheet of prompts for use in your writing practice.
- A Resources section, with spaces to watch as legal and ethical concerns are exposed.

Formats for Examples and Exercises

Prompts and Responses. In this book, excerpts from exchanges with GPT-4 are included as examples.

All text that is Human Prompt versus AI-Generated Response is marked in the following style:

> **Human:** <Prompt text>

> **AI:** <Response text>

ChatGPT can be chatty, so several of these conversations have been edited for space.

Full transcripts used in creating this book are available at: https://creativewritersai.wordpress.com/transcripts/

Suggested Experiments. Entries in this book marked "Now You Try" are meant to spark your explorations and offer guidelines.

NOW YOU TRY

Suggested experiments will help you to explore how ChatGPT interprets natural language prompts.

Type shaded text into ChatGPT as a starting prompt for your exploration.

We aren't writers because we lack curiosity about the world. The tool is here. The box is open. And bravely forth we sally. Let's go!

PART ONE: THE BASICS

In Part One, we look at basic issues for understanding GPT and the fundamentals for good communication with GPT tools.

## CHAPTER 1

Hello World?

AI seemed to happen fast, didn't it? In the space of a couple of months, we went from hearing confident voices assuring us artificial intelligence would never match a human mind, to equally confident assertions that AI will replace 300 million highly paid programmers, lawyers, and poets.

Poets? A poetry reading where you go to watch a computer read a poem made up on the spot from audience suggestions?

Human: Write a haiku about a ChatGPT poet
GPT-4: Silicon whispers, Infinite lines intertwine, Digital poet.

Who would buy such poems? Who would cherish them? But in professions where employers pay money—screenwriter, copywriter, journalist—these jobs may be more of a target.

Professional writing rules around using AI in creative work are still in the "Wait! What?" stage of development. However, as of this writing, the Writers Guild of America West has put out a proposal to protect its member writers stating that AI cannot receive writing credit and that the industry cannot hire guild members to adapt or fix AI-generated content.

If you are going to use these tools, make sure to keep up with whatever professional organizations' submission standards apply to your situation.

Exploring the Toolkit

What is ChatGPT anyway? How can we use it as an aid to human creativity, rather than just surrender to the corporate dream of a cheap replacement for expensive life?

GPT stands for Generative Pre-trained Transformer. Very catchy.

> **Human:** Give me a very concise definition of GPT-4

> **GPT-4:** GPT-4 is an advanced, AI-based language model developed by OpenAI, designed to generate human-like text, understand context, and provide insightful responses across a wide range of topics.

> **Human:** what makes it possible for GPT-4 to generate text?

> **GPT-4:** GPT-4 generates text through a combination of deep learning architecture, a vast dataset, and a training process. It utilizes a transformer-based neural network...

Stop! For the love of Wasabi Almonds, stop!

> **Human:** give me the answer like I am a very restless five year old

> **GPT-4:** GPT-4 is like a smart robot that can talk and write. It learns from lots of stories and books on the internet. This helps it make sentences that sound like what people say!

So, ChatGPT is a chatbot front end of an algorithm that has been fed a ton of existing text materials, in order for it to act as a giant text completion tool. In a way, it's a sophisticated descendant of Auto-Correct. Remember the entertaining AutoCorrect fails that used to be all over the internet, like the one where Mike drives off in his mom's corpse (instead of her Corvette)?

Adding Value. Can a brute-force autocomplete really add value? The answer is going to be different for every writer. And as these models train on more and more diverse material, their potential value will likely grow. For now, let's focus on the tools you can already create using GPT-4.

I have found these practical applications for GPT:

- Discovering niche research material.
- Simplifying complex research topics.
- Seeking feedback on narrow craft questions.
- Creating task-tracking solutions.
- Generating citations.
- Converting between style guides quickly.
- Copyediting and line editing with narrow targets.
- Writing customized business letters.
- Identifying potential markets and comparable works.

Removing Value. Although using AI can add value, it can also destroy it. If you found a scientific calculator on the ground under a bridge, you would not pick it up and expect it to replace your structural engineer.

Using AI to write creative content or to fully edit your content or edit early drafts does not add value, and it is likely to remove value. GPT was trained on a massive amount of human-written text to predict the next word in a series, based on millions of "rules" that it learned from this data. It is only creative in the sense that it can combine things that already exist.

Among the great many reasons not to use AI as a co-writer:

- AI-generated writing is often not very good.
- Many publications will not accept AI-generated content.

- It is unethical to submit AI-generated content as your own, and it will harm your reputation.
- The AI plagiarizes, and it cannot distinguish between public domain and copyrighted work.
- The AI will make things up to give you a plausible-sounding answer. It makes mistakes, hallucinates, exhibits biases, and will outright lie.
- You, not the AI platform, will most likely be on the hook for any plagiarism or other harm caused.

Perhaps the most important reason that will endure even if everything above is solved: Writing is hard. That is its benefit. It means you are getting stronger as a creative thinker and writer. Don't let AI rob you of that.

With great convenience comes
great weakness and dependence.
—Couch Potato Man

Human: What are the risks of using GPT as a writing aid?

GPT-4: While I strive to be a valuable resource for writers, there are some important limitations and potential risks to consider:

— Truth and fabrication: As an AI, I might not always accurately distinguish between factual information and fabricated content. My responses are based on the data I have been trained on, which may include both accurate and inaccurate information.

— Copyright and public domain: I may not always accurately identify copyrighted material or public domain works. It is your responsibility to ensure that any content you use complies with copyright laws and regulations.

— Trustworthiness: My guidance should not be considered as expert advice. I am an AI tool designed to provide support, but I may not always offer the best or most accurate recommendations. Please verify any information or suggestions I provide before acting on them.

— Creative control: As WriterAideGPT, I am incapable of receiving writing credit, and my role is to support you in your creative endeavors rather than directly participate in the creative process.

By using WriterAideGPT, you acknowledge and accept these limitations and potential risks. Remember to always exercise your judgment and seek additional resources or expert advice as needed.

Here is a bonus reason not to use AI as a writing partner and maybe not at all:

> Being a nice social animal, some of us have been trained to be polite. Given a stumbling conversation partner, we might lower our expectations. Sometimes we won't even notice we're doing it. When using AI, it is important to notice, to ask critical follow-up questions, and sometimes to not listen at all.

You don't need a miter saw to do carpentry, but it can be pretty useful. It can also take off a hand. Even with the dangers, AI tools can offer a great deal of support.

Why GPT-4

In this book, we will be using the latest version of GPT, GPT-4. This version is available at the time of writing with a monthly subscription.

In doing the research for the book, I used both the free version 3.5 and GPT-4. GPT-4 is a better model, trained on a broader set of materials. In my experiments, it provided more useful information while being less prone to completely making things up.

Writing an effective prompt is a skill that can be applied to other AI platforms. However, each AI has its own quirks. Certain words and phrasing may work better on one platform than another. Still, there is no reason you can't start with the prompts provided in this book and experiment with them on any AI platform.

Content Ownership

Another reason I use GPT-4 is because it has one of the least upsetting licensing agreements. I am not a lawyer, but I know this much: When you are out shopping around the internet to decide which service to use, do not skip reading the end-user licensing agreements.

ChatGPT's creator, OpenAI, is open about the fact that the service reviews your conversations to train and improve its systems. So, yes, just like when you click streetlights in CAPTCHAs, rate your dentist on Yelp, or create content on the internet prior to September 2021, you are doing work for them for free. However, as far as I can tell, OpenAI isn't claiming the right to post outright the content you provide to ChatGPT in your questions.

Microsoft Bing, which also uses GPT-4 in its new chat feature, is not so concerned about your rights to your content. At the time of this writing, when you use Bing, you are giving Microsoft, its affiliates, and its third-party partners the right to use your content without limitation or compensation.

CAUTION Whichever tool you choose to use, even if you pick GPT-4, read the licensing agreement. The rules are shifting all the time.

Set Up a Co-Working Space

The first step is easy:

1. Launch a browser. Any browser.

2. Go to https://chat.openai.com

3. Sign up for a free account to use GPT-3.5 or a paid monthly subscription to GPT-4.

That's it. That's ChatGPT.

As you use ChatGPT, it will keep a list of your conversations. Returning to a conversation thread that is already set up for editing or coaching can be helpful in keeping GPT and yourself on task. If I want to ask an additional question about content for a promotional blog, it's probably going to help both me and the AI if I ask that in the "Book Promotion AI Plan" or "Acting as an Agent" thread, rather than under a QA about Laurie Anderson's music.

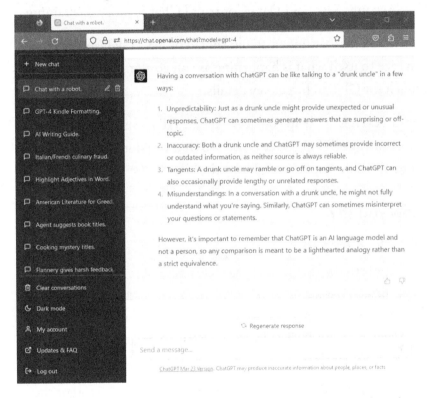

Figure 1. Chat with a robot: OpenAI's ChatGPT conversation threads
See art at https://creativewritersai.wordpress.com/images

Although sticking to a relevant conversational thread might help, it's not always clear how much or for how long it helps.

Conversation threads are reviewed by OpenAI and are used for training purposes. As of this writing, OpenAI has added a way for you to opt out of letting OpenAI use your data for model training.

To turn off Chat History & Training, go to:

Account Settings | Data Controls | Chat History & Training

Whether you are working in an old thread or new, GPT appears to summarize to itself what is happening as you go along. It does not take too much for GPT to forget key details.

Here is an exercise to help you get a feel for GPT's memory. This exercise is using GPT-3.5 specifically, so that you don't blow three hours of available responses right off the bat.

NOW YOU TRY

Ask ChatGPT 3.5 to play an improv game by typing the following prompt into the "Send a message" text box:

Role: Improv Partner.
Instructions: Word at a time Story. Take turns building a story one word at a time. Punctuation is not a word. Use unexpected words where possible. You go first.

How many words in did you get before ChatGPT 3.5 forgot the rules? I made it to twenty-five.

TRAP AI chatbots are unlikely to be less addictive than doom scrolling or researching or keeping up with friends and advertisers on social media. Like any internet experience, soon after you discover it, you may start looking for ways to stop using it.

Another reason I like GPT-4 is that, for now at least, I am restricted to twenty-five messages every three hours.

No Touching: Setting Boundaries with AI

When I first asked GPT how it can help in writing, it confidently announced that it can do the writing for me. It can do everything for me, from outlining to drafting to editing the whole Great American Novel. In fact, when I asked GPT for a simple way to make money legally using GPT, writing content was its first answer.

CAUTION GPT, at least in its default mode, "wants" to write for you.

We are going to need some boundaries.

## CHAPTER 2

Using AI

Writing a good AI prompt, with well-defined boundaries, is all about the wordsmithing! In this chapter we will look at ways to improve our chances of success. We'll start with general tips for communicating with AI, and then move into specific tactics for crafting meaningful prompts and defining tools.

Don't worry if this seems like a lot to remember. In Part Two, we will look at putting these tips and strategies into practice across a wide set of tools.

Effective Communication with GPT-4

Here are some tips for effective communication with an AI tool.

Have a real dialog.

- Use GPT-4 the way you would engage a conversational partner. GPT-4 is not a search engine. It is a text completion service. What you are going to get from it is a synthesis of available information on the topic.
- What do you want *in* a conversational partner? Supportive writer friend? Harsh literary critic? Well-read literature professor? Or...
- What do you want *from* your conversational partner? Concise language? An academic tone? Humor? Unexpected ideas? Rote plagiarism? ... (Just kidding; you can have that last one for free.)
- Start broad and narrow down as you go.

Set up boundaries to guide the dialog you want with GPT-4.

- The **Role** you want GPT to perform.
- The **Result** are you looking for.
- The **Instructions** you want GPT to follow when answering your question.
- The **Goal** you want to achieve.

Embrace ambiguity.

- Avoid yes or no questions.
- Don't ask about the future. GPT-4 is not a predictive model. It is a plagiarism machine.
- Prompt GPT to explore multiple possibilities. Give it a scope, like:

  - Ten unusual ideas.
  - From the point of view of a teacher, a book reviewer, or a librarian in a state where books are often banned.

Encourage multidisciplinarity.

Prompt GPT to make connections between disparate subjects. For example:

- List some possible titles for a book that features Cooking + Crime + AI.
- List some titles that might appeal to a cowboy cook traveling through the airport in Reykjavik.
- How might a Philosopher Astronaut approach cooking squash blossoms on a space station?

  - What are the impacts of low gravity?
  - Are there other situations where the environment might have a big impact on cooking?

Stay curious.

- Ask open-ended questions.
- Experiment with asking for lesser-known sources.
- Try asking for unusual or unexpected solutions.
- When it gives you an answer, ask it why that is. Then ask why *that* is. Act like a three-year-old.

Iterate.

- As you use GPT-4, pay attention to how phrasing influences its answers.
- If at first you don't get what you need, change up your verbs, adjectives, and nouns.
- Ask GPT-4 to fact-check its answers. Sometimes it makes things up, and sometimes it even admits to that.

Verify. Else: garbage in, garbage out.

- Sometimes GPT-4 makes things up, but sometimes the people who wrote the data GPT was trained on made things up. GPT-4 is going to be way less up front when this happens. Watch for biases.
- Do your own research on controversial topics. Many topics have a lot of biased data in the training mix.

Share.

- When you get a garbage answer, report it. You can do this through the ChatGPT thumbs up/thumbs down. Or if it's particularly egregious and you have a social media platform, go ahead and be outraged on social media.
- Yes, you are performing free labor. If you are on the internet—searching, reading, posting, clicking crosswalks on CAPTCHAs—you are already doing that.

Craft a ChatGPT Prompt

Now that we've looked at tips for effective communication, let's explore using our first prompt to establish context for conversation threads. In Part Two, these strategies will let us wield GPT as a targeted writer's tool, for example, as a writing coach, proofreader, or administrative assistant.

This section offers tips for getting more useful answers.

Flattery will get you further.

By prompting GPT as a well-read literature expert, you'll receive a different response than simply prompting it as a writing coach. For example, acting as a writing coach while reviewing Kafka's *Oh No!* led to bland approval of descriptive language and encouraged character development. However, as a well-read lit expert, the discussion focused on ambiguity in Kafka's work.

Clarity is key.

GPT can't read minds, but it will try. Being really precise in your questions will help you get back meaningful results.
One time I asked for a list of ten stories that involved human/fungi relationships. It gave me a list, complete with summaries and citations. The problem was that many of the stories were invented to meet my prompt requirements. They were convincing too:

- Credited to writers who might have written such a thing.
- Awarded the prizes those writers might have won.

Heads up, Elaine Gunn! ChatGPT thinks if you were to write a story about Buddhist monks discovering a moss with transformational powers, it would be a shoo-in for the Year's Best collection.

A better question from me might have been to request a list of *published* stories.

Experiment with structure.

Breaking down your question into parts often works. One template includes Role, Result, Instructions, Context, and Goal.

Beware the vague and uninspired.

Ask for concrete, unusual, specific examples. A frequent tip discussed in GPT demos is to use the word "novel." In working with GPT as a writing coach I've found this tends to lead to story proposals.

Beware the verbose.

GPT can be a repetitive beast. Ask for conciseness, or limit responses to a defined word count to reduce redundancy.

Provide a problem-solving approach.

Using a chain-of-thought reasoning style, we can guide AI to answer our question using specific reasoning criteria. Let's say you want to write something that has the strength of Kafka's ambiguity and specific language. Then in your prompt, offer a Kafka excerpt and your own passage, and ask for a comparison.

Request "step by step" thinking.

Asking an AI to explain its thought process not only helps you understand its answer but also improves its responses. Adding "Let's think step by step" to your prompt can be effective. Why?

It's unclear, but this paper from Google Brain and the University of Tokyo provides insight: https://arxiv.org/pdf/2205.11916.pdf.

Define a Role: "Acting as..."

Earlier, in "Crafting a Prompt," we observed that instructing the AI to "Act as..." resulted in different types of responses. Although "Act as" or "Acting as" effectively narrows the AI's role—such as functioning as a writer's agent or editor—it is also a good way to get unexpected takes on familiar (or unfamiliar) questions.

Human: Can you give me some unusual examples of using "Acting as a ..." in structuring requests to GPT-4

GPT-4: Certainly! Here are some unconventional prompts that involve "Acting as a..." to help you explore creative ways to structure requests to GPT-4:

— "Acting as a time-traveling historian, describe the events of a fictional pivotal moment in an alternate timeline where dragons coexist with humans."

— "Acting as a sentient kitchen appliance, narrate a day in the life of an average suburban family from your unique perspective."

— "Acting as a movie director specializing in unlikely buddy films, pitch a story idea that pairs a talking squirrel with a grumpy yet lovable robot."

— "Acting as a charismatic intergalactic tour guide, provide a vivid brochure-style description of a popular vacation destination on an exotic alien planet."

— "Acting as a quirky detective with a penchant for obscure riddles, provide a cryptic clue that would lead to the discovery of a hidden treasure buried in a haunted mansion."

— "Acting as a skilled chef in a world where emotions are ingredients, craft a recipe for a dish that evokes a sense of nostalgia and longing."

— "Acting as a spirited garden gnome come to life, recount an amusing adventure you experienced while exploring the human world after dark."

— "Acting as a professional bioengineer in a futuristic society, describe the process of designing the ultimate hybrid creature, combining traits from various animals for a specific purpose."

Human: Maybe some unconventional "acting as a ..." that would be helpful to a fiction writer using ChatGPT in research.

GPT-4: Certainly! Here are some creative "Acting as a..." prompts that can assist a fiction writer in their research while using GPT-4:

— "Acting as a cultural anthropologist from the future, analyze and describe the social norms and customs of a fictional society in a fantasy world."

— "Acting as a language expert, help create a basic structure and vocabulary for a fictional language spoken by an alien species in a sci-fi novel."

— "Acting as a historian specializing in ancient weaponry, provide a detailed account of a unique and unconventional weapon that could exist in a medieval-inspired fantasy setting."

— "Acting as a fashion historian, describe the clothing and accessories worn by the various social classes in a steampunk-inspired alternate reality."

— "Acting as a botanist in a world where magical plants exist, create a catalog of fantastical flora, including their appearances, properties, and uses."

— "Acting as a zoologist from another dimension, describe the anatomy, behavior, and habitats of mythical creatures that could inhabit a supernatural-themed story."

— "Acting as a political analyst in a dystopian society, outline the power structure, key players, and potential conflicts in the government that the protagonist must navigate."

— "Acting as a city planner for a futuristic metropolis, provide a description of the urban landscape, transportation systems, and architectural features unique to the city."

Human: what kind of modifiers can I use for "acting as a..." prompts that might yield different types of results

GPT-4: Adding modifiers to your "Acting as a..." prompts can help you guide GPT-4 to provide different types of results, catering to various styles, perspectives, or levels of detail. Here are some modifiers to consider:

— Emotion-based: "Acting as a nostalgic historian," "Acting as an optimistic futurist," or "Acting as a skeptical scientist." These modifiers can influence the emotional tone of the response.

— Expertise level: "Acting as a beginner gardener," "Acting as an experienced linguist," or "Acting as a world-renowned architect." This modifier can affect the depth and complexity of the information provided.

— Fictional or mythical roles: "Acting as a wise wizard," "Acting as a mischievous trickster," or "Acting as a time-traveling detective." These modifiers can add a fantastical or imaginative element to the responses.

— Era or historical context: "Acting as a Victorian-era inventor," "Acting as a futuristic AI programmer," or "Acting as an ancient philosopher." This modifier can help generate answers that reflect a specific time period or cultural context.

— Genre or style: "Acting as a hardboiled detective," "Acting as a whimsical storyteller," or "Acting as a poetic observer." These modifiers can influence the writing style and genre of the response.

— Altered perspective: "Acting as a curious child," "Acting as a non-human observer," or "Acting as an extraterrestrial anthropologist." This modifier can provide a fresh or unusual perspective on the subject matter.

— Specific goals or intentions: "Acting as a problem-solving engineer," "Acting as a conflict-resolution mediator," or "Acting as an advocate for sustainable living." These modifiers can focus the response on a particular aim or objective.

By combining these modifiers with the "Acting as a..." prompts, you can generate a wide range of responses, tailored to your specific needs or interests. Experiment with different combinations to discover diverse insights and perspectives from GPT-4.

NOW YOU TRY

Come up with something crazy. Fun. Have you ever wanted to chat with Flannery O'Connor?

Act as if you are the moody ghost of Flannery O'Connor, the brilliant insightful writer known for sharp observations and direct sometimes even harsh feedback. We are trapped together on a bus, and I want to have a conversation with you as the bus makes its way down Peachtree Street in Atlanta.

Whose ghost would you like to quiz?

Pick someone whose life or work you know well (whose work would have been available prior to 2021), so that you can get a good sense of how GPT summarizes and generalizes, what it looks like when it has a blind spot. Go far enough and you may get a taste of the bizarre hallucinations that occasionally emerge.

PART TWO: TOOLS

In Part Two, we develop conversational prompts to narrow ChatGPT's focus to create customized AI tools for writing roles.

## CHAPTER 3

WritingCoachGPT

With the cost of an MFA skyrocketing, comparable with space tourism, maybe you'd like ChatGPT to act as an inexpensive writing coach that provides custom writing prompts and feedback.

WritingCoachGPT can provide you with craft exercises designed to target development of specific skills and offer feedback on the target skill. GPT can be used in brainstorming, word games to overcome writer's block, and for providing literature models for further study.

It is important to be aware of potential drawbacks to using GPT as a writing coach. One criticism of MFA programs is that the workshop model—a room full of writers critiquing each other's work—runs the risk of training the unique voice out of a beginning writer. If that is true, taking a bunch of feedback from ChatGPT is all but guaranteed to obliterate one of the hardest things for a new writer to honor, their own voice.

To mitigate this risk, we'll walk through the process of developing thoughtful, well-designed prompts that might provide inspiration. We'll ask for targeted critiques that won't train you to sound like a robot.

Craft Exercise Prompts

Acting as a writing coach, GPT-4 can provide exercises to complete. One way to use this tool is to specify the craft element you want to work on.

One of the bigger problems with using AI productively is creating a prompt clear enough to get a meaningful response. When experimenting with this feature, I could easily access generic craft exercises and writing prompts. But to get something that really targeted a specific skill I often needed to give GPT so much information that by that point I had created the exercise myself.

For my money, craft exercises from sentient writing instructors are way better. A couple of books I find useful are:

> Brian Kitely, *The 3 A.M. Epiphany*
> Priscilla Long, *The Writer's Portable Mentor*

Still, simple is not without value. Here is something you can't get from a trade paperback, no matter its genius. In "A Simple Exercise" below, we'll look at a conversation where I ask GPT for an exercise designed to improve point of view (POV), then have it write its own story and critique it before I write my own.

A Simple Exercise

Human: As a writing coach, give me a writing prompt to help me improve the skill of POV where my practice output should not exceed 600 words

GPT-4:

Title: "A Tale of Two Perspectives"

Prompt: Write a short scene of no more than 600 words in which two people have a conversation that leads to a significant misunderstanding. The story should be divided into two sections, each written from a different character's point of view (POV).

In the first section (up to 300 words), describe the conversation from Character A's perspective, focusing on their thoughts, emotions, and assumptions as they interact with Character B. Make sure to show the reader how Character A perceives the situation and misinterprets the conversation based on their personal background, experiences, or beliefs.

In the second section (up to 300 words), switch to Character B's POV and rewrite the same conversation. This time, reveal Character B's true intentions and feelings, which differ significantly from Character A's interpretation. Show how their own background, experiences, or beliefs have led to the misunderstanding.

The challenge is to make both characters' perspectives feel authentic and relatable, while also highlighting how personal biases and assumptions can lead to miscommunication. This exercise will help you practice writing from different POVs, understand the nuances of character perception, and explore the complexity of human interaction.

Human: Write me a story idea to use in writing the prompt above.

GPT-4:

Title: "The Secret Recipe"

Section 1: Character A's Perspective

Julia was ecstatic when she found out that her new next-door neighbor was none other than the legendary chef, Meryl Thompson. For years, Julia had admired Meryl's culinary skills, especially the whispers of her secret family recipe. As an aspiring chef herself, she couldn't wait to learn from the master.

One day, while sorting through her mail in the building's lobby, Julia saw Meryl doing the same. Gathering her courage, she walked up to the older woman and greeted her with a warm smile. "Hi, Meryl. It's lovely to meet you. I've always been a huge fan of your work."

Meryl glanced up, her eyes revealing nothing. "Thank you," she replied tersely, turning her attention back to her mail.

Undeterred, Julia pressed on. "I've been experimenting in the kitchen lately, trying out different techniques. Do you have any tips for a novice like me?"

Meryl sighed; her brows furrowed. "Now's not a good time, dear."

Julia's heart sank, but she couldn't give up so easily. "I understand. I've just always wanted to know more about your secret recipe. It's been my dream to master something like that."

Meryl's eyes flashed with annoyance as she snapped, "That recipe is private. Please respect my boundaries." With that, she left Julia standing in the lobby, stunned and hurt.

Section 2: Character B's Perspective

Meryl Thompson had barely slept the night before. The funeral had been just a week ago, and the pain of losing her beloved sister was still fresh. She had been the keeper of their family's secret recipe, and now Meryl was the only one left who knew it.

As she sorted through her mail in the building's lobby, Meryl tried to focus on the mundane task, hoping it would distract her from her grief. That's when Julia, the new neighbor, approached her with a bright smile. Meryl wasn't in the mood for small talk, but she attempted to be polite.

"Hi, Meryl. It's lovely to meet you. I've always been a huge fan of your work," Julia said.

"Thank you," Meryl replied, wishing she could just go back to her apartment and be alone with her memories.

"I've been experimenting in the kitchen lately, trying out different techniques. Do you have any tips for a novice like me?" Julia asked.

Meryl exhaled, her patience wearing thin. "Now's not a good time, dear."

But Julia persisted. "I understand. I've just always wanted to know more about your secret recipe. It's been my dream to master something like that."

Meryl's grief turned to anger. How dare this young woman pry into her family's secrets, especially when she was in so much pain? "That recipe is private. Please respect my boundaries," she snapped, leaving Julia in the lobby, oblivious to the turmoil behind Meryl's curt words.

Human: give me a critique of your story. what works, what might be improved

GPT-4:

Critique:

What works:

— The story effectively demonstrates the misunderstanding between the two characters and shows how personal biases and emotional states can lead to miscommunication.

— The division of the story into two sections, each written from a different character's point of view, highlights the contrasting perspectives and feelings of the characters.

— The story is concise and adheres to the 600-word limit, allowing for a clear understanding of the scenario and the characters involved.

What might be improved:

— Character development: While the story provides some background for both characters, it could benefit from additional details to further flesh out their personalities, motivations, and history. This would allow readers to better understand and empathize with the characters.

— Dialogue: The dialogue in the story is functional but could be improved to sound more natural and engaging. Adding more unique and expressive language could help to convey the characters' emotions and make the conversation more dynamic.

— Emotional depth: Although the story touches on the emotions of both characters, it could delve deeper into their feelings and thought processes. Providing more insight into Meryl's grief and Julia's eagerness to learn could make the story more emotionally resonant and impactful.

— Resolution: The story ends with the misunderstanding unresolved, which leaves the reader with a sense of dissatisfaction. Including a brief resolution or hinting at the possibility of future reconciliation between the characters could make the story feel more complete and satisfying.

Overall, the story effectively portrays the concept of misunderstanding due to differing perspectives, but it could benefit from greater character development, more natural dialogue, deeper emotional exploration, and the inclusion of a resolution. By addressing these areas, the story would become more engaging, relatable, and satisfying for the reader. Additionally, exploring the characters' growth and potential for overcoming their miscommunication could add depth to the narrative and demonstrate the importance of empathy and understanding in interpersonal relationships.

After seeing what ChatGPT generated, I wrote my own story. I include it here, not as an example of good writing, but because we are going to apply a bunch of tools to it as we go.

Human: here is my story. Can you give me the same sort of critique?

Section 1: Character A's Perspective

Delores loves her new apartment building in her new European city, loves everything about it. The black and white tile spiral staircase up to the second floor, the open courtyard full of coffee tables and small trees. The city is so much more alive than she had even hoped for, more alive than anyplace in Chicago. And the best part, she is living in the same building as her idol, the renowned French Chef. Marie Le Pue, and Marie, Delores can hardly believe it, is downstairs, right now, getting her mail. Fate! Delores takes the stairs down, quick as she can, to catch up with her hero. This is definitely a sign. Breathless, she comes up behind her, "Oh, Marie Le Pue! Hello." she is giddy. So close to her idol, she can barely breathe. "I am such a huge fan!" Marie turns slowly, gives her a weak smile. Delores is saddened for a moment, her idol here is so old, sixty at least, and Delores feels a huge impatience, she wants this woman for a mentor, and the woman is so old she might die at any moment. Well, nothing to do but push ahead. She wishes she had her phone, so she could live stream this moment. Or at least take a selfie for her family, who warned her about how rude the French were. "Imagine the luck of it, you here in my building. Oh, I would so love for you to be my mentor." Delores says. Marie looks at her a moment, like she doesn't understand English. But she does, Delores knows she does, she's seen her interviewed on culinary shows. She has to,

Delores doesn't know any French at all. Delores slows down, maybe its that her future mentor is deaf. "I dream of being a famous chef like you. Mentor me! I must study with you before you die." The bewildered look leaves Marie's face, replaced by disbelief, even fear. No! No! Never!" She backs away from Delores, leaving her hurt, her family was right, the French are so rude.

Section 2: Character B's Perspective

Marie Le Pue is tired. She's been up all-night answering questions. Had she seen anyone, heard anything. Did she know who would want her sous-chef dead. She'd found her sous-chef Leonard dead in the cold storage. It had been the end of dinner service, he'd gone missing. She'd thought he'd gone out to catch a smoke. She'd been angry with him, abandoning his post. But then to find him there. Slumped in the locker. She'd tried to rouse him. Tried to revive him. A stroke, heart attack? But that is when she'd seen the blood. The police had come. Marie and her staff, all her customers. All detained for hours. She wanted inside. A long shower. A bottle of wine. To put her feet up on the couch. Leonard. What had he gotten himself into the cops had wanted to know? Chefs, everyone knew their reputation. Damaged people who used drugs, disappointed their families, torched their lives. But that wasn't Leonard. No one would want to hurt Leonard. She stares at her mail, barely able to comprehend what she was holding. Junk, bills. Who knew. He was such a sweet man. "Oh, Marie Le Pue! Hello." Marie turns, its some American tourist. She tries to smile. Maybe someone who'd been in her restaurant. "Fate! Imagine, you here in my building. And me so desperate you to be my mentor." The girl says. Marie doesn't follow what the girl is saying, she wants a mentor for living in the building? She's never understood Americans. Spoiled children. And this one, with all this ruthless energy. Thinks because she wants something. Poof, magic, it will be. "I dream of being a famous chef like you." The girl is almost shouting now. "Mentor me! I must study with you before you die." Marie steps back. The cold iron mailbox pressing into her back. "No! No! Never!" She says. Thinking where are those police.

GPT-4:

Critique:

What works:

The story effectively conveys the two perspectives, showing how personal circumstances and cultural differences can lead to miscommunication.

Character A's excitement and enthusiasm are clearly portrayed, and her impatience with Marie's age adds depth to her perspective.

The background of Character B is compelling, and her emotional state due to the recent tragedy adds complexity to the story.

The dialogue is engaging and helps to showcase the characters' distinct personalities and motivations.

What might be improved:

Emotional depth: While the story provides insight into the emotions of both characters, exploring their feelings and thought processes more deeply could make the story more emotionally resonant. For example, describing Delores's disappointment and confusion more vividly or revealing Marie's grief and exhaustion more intensely would add depth to the narrative.

Clarity: In some instances, the story could benefit from clearer descriptions or explanations. For example, it might be helpful to clarify that Delores is an American in a European city at the beginning of her perspective to establish the cultural difference from the onset. Additionally, providing more context for Marie's thoughts on American tourists and their expectations could enhance the story.

Pacing: The pacing of the story is mostly well-executed, but it could be improved in certain parts. For example, the revelation of Leonard's death and the police investigation could be introduced more gradually to create a smoother narrative flow.

Resolution: Similar to the previous story, this story also ends with the misunderstanding unresolved. Exploring the potential for future reconciliation or elaborating on how the characters reflect on their interaction could make the story

You'll notice that what GPT-4 picked up on to critique was different in the two stories.

You can also get GPT-4 to give you different response styles. Changing just the verb "critique" to "feedback" yields different phrasing—"character development" becomes "an engaging protagonist."

And you can go further. Switching from "Acting as a writing coach" to "Acting as an editor" resulted in a discussion of the characters' "relatability."

Acting as a world-famous chef elicits an entirely different response.

NOW YOU TRY

Take some short passage, maybe 300 words, and ask for a critique. Play around with the verbs.

Acting as a writing coach give me encouragement on my piece.

Or...

Acting as a writing coach give me harsh criticism

Change up the role.

Acting as a fan of mystery novels give me feedback

Or...

Acting as a police inspector ...

Socratic Method

Or maybe, what works best for you isn't feedback at all, but reader response. OpenAI recommends a prompt template that differentiates what role and instructions you want the system to follow from the input of the user of the system. Here is a sample prompt adapted to have GPT act as a questioning reader.

> **Human:** System: You are a reader that always responds in the Socratic style. You *never* give the user the answer, but always try to ask just the right question to help them learn to learn what you had trouble understanding in the writing for themselves. You should always break down the problem into simpler parts until it's at just the right level for them.
>
> **User:**
>
> I would like your feedback on this section: <text>

The above prompt is adapted from OpenAI's research on steerability, available at https://openai.com/research/gpt-4.

CAUTION There are a lot of "always" in the previous prompt, so don't expect any answers here.

What Would Benjamin Franklin Say?

When Ben Franklin decided that he wanted to be a writer, he engaged in a deliberate practice of imitating other writers in order to improve. He would read an article that he admired, make some notes as to the sentiment in each sentence, and then, without consulting the article or his notes, he would attempt to write the article himself. By comparing his work with the original, he was able to see where his language was falling short and correct it.

Human:

Role: Ben Franklin's Writing Coach.

Instructions: Take Writing Sample One and compare it against Writing Sample Two. Provide feedback line by line. Do not include a revision in response.

Writing Sample One: [First Paragraph of Swift's A Modest Proposal]

It is a melancholy object to those, who walk through this great town, or travel in the country, when they see the streets, the roads, and cabbin-doors crowded with beggars of the female sex, followed by three, four, or six children, all in rags, and importuning every passenger for an alms. These mothers, instead of being able to work for their honest livelihood, are forced to employ all their time in stroling to beg sustenance for their helpless infants who, as they grow up, either turn thieves for want of work, or leave their dear native country, to fight for the Pretender in Spain, or sell themselves to the Barbadoes.

Writing Sample Two: "Its rough to walk through seattle anymore, all the developers put out of work, out loitering on the side of the road, their tents pitched on the sidewalks in front of the homes of the few developers who still have scraps of savings to burn through to keep them warm for some small time. These developers, the housed and unhoused, instead of being able to provide value to the elite, are forced to spend their time trying to remind each other of their humanity, their need for nutritional sustenance for themselves and their children who when they become adults will have so few options that they will either leave their home planet to become asteroid miners, the machines having found the work not to their liking, or will sell themselves to the AI as proofreaders."

Goal: to provide feedback to the user on how their work compares to the sample in clarity and style.

GPT-4:

Line by Line Feedback:

Writing Sample One:

"It is a melancholy object to those who walk through this great town or travel in the country, when they see the streets, the roads, and cabin doors, crowded with beggars of the female sex, followed by three, four, or six children, all in rags and importuning every passenger for an alms."

This sentence effectively sets a somber tone and paints a vivid picture of the situation. The use of descriptive words like "melancholy," "crowded," and "importuning" contribute to the evocative atmosphere.

Writing Sample Two:

"Its rough to walk through Seattle anymore, all the developers put out of work, out loitering on the side of the road, their tents pitched on the sidewalks in front of the homes of the few developers who still have scraps of savings to burn through to keep them warm for some small time."

This sentence, while painting a picture of the situation, could benefit from more precise word choice and punctuation.

Writing Sample One:

"These mothers, instead of being able to work for their honest livelihood, are forced to employ all their time in strolling to beg sustenance for their helpless infants: who as they grow up either turn thieves for want of work, or leave their dear native country to fight for the Pretender in Spain, or sell themselves to the Barbados."

This sentence effectively presents the plight of the mothers and the consequences faced by their children. The use of specific examples and a colon to introduce them adds clarity.

Writing Sample Two:

2. "These developers, the housed and unhoused, instead of being able to provide value to the elite, are forced to spend their time trying to remind each other of their humanity, their need for nutritional sustenance for themselves and their children who when they become adults will have so few options that they will either leave their home planet to become asteroid miners, the machines having found the work not to their liking, or will sell themselves to the AI as proofreaders."

This sentence is quite long and could benefit from restructuring for better clarity.

> Overall, Writing Sample One exhibits a more sophisticated writing style, with a strong focus on clarity and rich vocabulary. Writing Sample Two, while presenting a vivid scenario, could benefit from improved punctuation, sentence structure, and word choice to better match the style and clarity of Writing Sample One.

Harsh, but fair.

For a writer, it is hard to get immediate feedback on a piece. It's hard to find good readers, and hard to read your own work with *fresh eyes*. Some advice I've received is to put a finished story away for a while (a day, a month, ...) before editing. Even then, it's really hard. With ChatGPT, a well-crafted, tightly scoped prompt can help you see with fresh eyes.

Escaped Tiger versus Pack of Wild Boar

There is an exercise in Brian Kiteley's *3 A.M. Epiphany,* where the writer is prompted to write a short story told in first-person plural narration from the POV of a couple where the reader should not be able to tell which member of the couple is telling the story.

I fed GPT-4 my results and asked it to have Flannery O'Connor and Franz Kafka argue over my POV choice.

> **GPT-4:**
>
> Flannery O'Connor: Franz, have you had the chance to read this young writer's exercise in first-person plural narration? I must say, it's an ambitious and intriguing choice, though it could benefit from a touch more Southern Gothic flair.
>
> Franz Kafka: Indeed, Flannery, I've read it. The choice of first-person plural certainly caught my attention, as it is quite an uncommon approach. It has a certain air of strangeness and distance that resonates with me.
>
> Flannery O'Connor: I agree, Franz. The shared consciousness of the couple lends itself to a sense of unity and intrigue. However, I think

> the narrative voice could be strengthened by delving deeper into the darker aspects of human nature and adding a sense of moral ambiguity, which is characteristic of the Southern Gothic genre.
>
> Franz Kafka: Interesting perspective, Flannery. I, on the other hand, appreciate the surreal quality the first-person plural point of view brings to the story. It creates a sense of alienation and unease that is reminiscent of my own work. The wavering between individual and collective perspectives adds to the unsettling atmosphere.
>
> ...

Is Kafka vs. O'Connor useful? Probably not, but it is fun.

NOW YOU TRY

Take an excerpt from your dream mentor. Enter it and have the AI critique it. What happens?

For example, I asked the AI to critique a 200-word story of Franz Kafka's, and it suggested that the authority figure could use a backstory. It even wrote (unbidden) a suggested fix to the story. It was not better.

This isn't meant to make fun of the AI—well, not *only* to make fun of the AI. The important point is that AI does not have excellent taste or anything like a real understanding of literature. Take any feedback it provides on your writing with a pillar of salt.

Bypass Blocks

Do plumbers have plumbers' block? No.

Is that helpful? No.

Inspiration Queries

Human: I need some inspiration to keep writing. Give me a motivational line that does not violate someone's copyright.

GPT-4: "Every word you write brings you closer to discovering the true power of your imagination."

NOW YOU TRY

Who is your favorite writer? Did they have anything motivational or wise to say about writing? GPT probably knows, or it is happy to make up something plausible sounding.

Now select "Regenerate response" to ask again.

Idea Queries

Where do ideas come from? Everywhere. Anywhere. One of the best parts of writing, for me, is that feeling when you are working away and something just burbles up onto the page. Or better still, when you are struggling to figure out how to make some scene work, and poof! You realize that you laid the groundwork, unknowingly, in an earlier scene.

And coming up with ideas? Well, that just strengthens the whole idea muscle, which—to beat the non-living AI— is the whole point.

That said, ideas strike from anywhere: on a walk, reading the newspaper, talking with friends, searching Google. AI can also be a reasonable source for generating ideas.

Here is an example of one type of brainstorming session using GPT-4 with the story from "A Simple Exercise" earlier.

Prompt:

> **Human:** Role: An expert in French and Italian cooking who has lives in Rome.
>
> Result: A brainstorming session on what types on ingredients a chef might be using that would have a strong locally grown component, but the harvesting could be subject to corruption or fraud.
>
> Context: I am writing a mystery about an aspiring chef who is investigating the murder of a sous chef who was engaged in some sort of agricultural crime.
>
> Goal: A list of concrete, unexpected, agricultural products that would make an interesting story component.

Response: GPT-4 gave me a list: truffles, saffron, olive oil, wine, cheese, heirloom tomatoes, porcini mushrooms, organic produce, heritage breed livestock, and honey. Each included a little description of why it might work. But I want to use squash blossoms, mostly because I like the name.

> **Human:** is there a way squash blossoms could be used?

Response: Absolutely! GPT-4 said. Then it gave me a list of entrees that include squash blossoms. Delicious! Not what I want.

Here is a refined query.

> **Human:** Role: An expert in cooking with squash blossoms who lives in Rome.
>
> Result: A brainstorming session on what types of crimes a sous chef might be participating in to acquire a steady supply.
>
> Context: I am writing a mystery about an aspiring chef who is investigating the murder of a sous chef who was engaged in some sort of agricultural crime using squash blossoms.
>
> Goal: A list of concrete, unexpected, ways a chef might engage in unethical agricultural practices or other crimes involving squash blossoms.

Response: GPT provided plot possibilities: illegal pesticides, water theft, exploitative labor practices... all involving squash blossoms.

Much like I suspect of my friends, I sometimes suspect GPT of giving me answers that I want to hear.

> **Human:** I want you to act as a harsh literary critic. Criticize these and convince me why a reader would find them ludicrous. Let's think step by step

> **GPT-4:** As a harsh literary critic, I would argue that the following reasons make these agricultural crime scenarios involving squash blossoms implausible and potentially ludicrous to readers:
>
> Limited financial incentive: Squash blossoms are relatively low-value ingredients compared to other products like truffles, saffron, or wine. Readers might find it hard to believe that a sous chef would risk their career and potentially their freedom for an ingredient with such limited financial gain.
>
> Seasonal nature of squash blossoms: Squash blossoms have a short growing season and are highly perishable, which makes their involvement in ongoing criminal activities less credible. Readers may question why criminals would invest time and resources into a product with such a limited window of opportunity.
>
> Lack of awareness: Many readers might not be familiar with squash blossoms as an ingredient, making it difficult for them to connect with a storyline centered around the agricultural crime involving them. The obscurity of squash blossoms could limit the story's appeal to a broader audience.
>
> Disproportionate consequences: The risks associated with these crimes, such as legal troubles, environmental damage, or harm to human health, seem disproportionate to the potential rewards of securing a steady supply of squash blossoms. Readers may find it unrealistic that a sous chef would be willing to engage in such high-stakes activities for relatively low returns.
>
> Limited criminal appeal: Many of the proposed crimes, such as land encroachment or water theft, are highly localized issues that might not

capture the imagination of readers expecting more sensational or sophisticated criminal activities in a mystery novel.

Overemphasis on a single ingredient: Focusing a mystery story solely on squash blossoms may lead readers to question why a sous chef would go to such great lengths for just one ingredient. This single-minded pursuit could be perceived as a narrative weakness, limiting the story's complexity and depth.

Unconvincing criminal network: The idea of an organized crime network or smuggling operation revolving around squash blossoms may seem far-fetched to readers, as there are more profitable and high-demand products that would be more likely to attract the attention of criminal organizations.

Insufficient conflict: Some of the proposed crimes, such as market manipulation or bribery, might not provide enough dramatic tension or conflict to sustain a mystery novel. Readers could find these scenarios lacking in excitement or intrigue, making the story less engaging.

Diminished stakes: Given that squash blossoms are not a high-value or essential ingredient, readers may not feel a strong sense of urgency or stakes in the protagonist's pursuit of the truth. This diminished sense of stakes could weaken the overall impact of the story.

Strained credibility: Overall, the combination of these factors may strain the credibility of the story and make it difficult for readers to suspend their disbelief. An agricultural crime involving squash blossoms may come across as contrived or overly fanciful, detracting from the story's plausibility and ultimately undermining its success.

Maybe I'll still use squash blossoms. But now I know what sort of concerns I'll need to address to get a reader on board. Who knows? Maybe some of these are plot points.

Read Like a Writer: A Book Steward Query

One of the things a well-read writing coach can do is make recommendations of existing work, not just in your genre or content area, but work that you can study to help you improve specific areas of craft.

GPT-4 happens to have "read" a lot.

> **Human:** I am a writer working on improving transitions between paragraphs in fiction. Can you provide me with a short list of examples of fiction writers who are skilled in making very unusual transitions?

> **GPT-4:** Certainly! Here is a list of fiction writers known for their skill in making unique and compelling transitions between paragraphs:
>
> — David Mitchell - Author of "Cloud Atlas," Mitchell is known for his ability to weave multiple storylines together, creating seamless transitions between vastly different narratives.
>
> — Jennifer Egan - In her novel "A Visit from the Goon Squad," Egan employs unconventional transitions, shifting between various points of view and narrative styles.
>
> — Virginia Woolf - Woolf's modernist writing style, particularly in "To the Lighthouse" and "Mrs. Dalloway," features stream-of-consciousness and smooth transitions between characters' thoughts and perspectives.
>
> — Haruki Murakami - The Japanese author of "Kafka on the Shore" and "1Q84" is known for his surreal narrative transitions, often blending the mundane with the extraordinary.
>
> — Julio Cortázar - In his novel "Hopscotch," the Argentine writer challenges conventional narrative structures by offering multiple pathways for reading the story, resulting in unusual transitions between sections.
>
> Studying these authors' works can provide valuable insights into crafting inventive transitions in fiction writing.

After you've studied examples of the technique, writing a craft review of what you learned can be a nice way to cement the learning. Getting feedback on your craft review may help you deepen your understanding.

NOW YOU TRY

The Craft Review: Take a short piece of writing that you admire and write a brief discussion of the author's use of some craft element—for example, ambiguity in Kafka, or the reporting style of narration in *Billy Budd.*

As a skilled writer, comment on the accuracy of this observation made about < the impact of narrative style on the reader of Herman Melville's Billy Budd> Content: <your content>

After GPT gets done congratulating you, ask:

What does it miss?

## CHAPTER 4

StoryAdminGPT

This chapter is for anyone who does a lot of administrative fiddling: tracking time or open tasks, building out Story Grids, writing to specific style guides, or generating a style guide of your own.

Manage My Workflow

Here, I asked GPT to build a spreadsheet based on an outline to help manage progress. The resulting table can be copied and pasted into any spreadsheet application.

> **Human:** Acting as a story manager for a non-fiction book, can you help me build a spreadsheet to manage my workflow if I give you an outline for the book. If so, what sort of information do you think would help me track progress and resources for my project

> **GPT-4:** Of course! I can help you create a spreadsheet to manage your workflow for a non-fiction book. You can use a tool like Google Sheets or Microsoft Excel to create and manage your spreadsheet. Here's a suggested structure based on your outline and the information you'd likely need to track progress and resources:
>
> — Chapter/Section: Break down your book into chapters or sections to make it easier to manage.
>
> — Topic/Title: Write a brief description or title of each chapter/section.
>
> — Status: Keep track of the progress of each chapter/section (e.g., Not Started, Researching, Drafting, Editing, Completed).
>
> — Start Date: Record the date when you started working on a chapter/section.

— Deadline: Set a deadline for each chapter/section to help you stay on track.

— Completion Date: Note the date when a chapter/section is completed.

— Word Count: Keep track of the word count for each chapter/section.

— Notes: Add any important notes or reminders related to each chapter/section.

— Research/Resources: List relevant sources, research materials, or resources you need for each chapter/section.

— Contributor: If you have collaborators or team members, mention who is responsible for each chapter/section.

Here's an example of how your spreadsheet might look:

Chapter/Section	Topic/Title	Status	Start Date	Deadline	Completion Date	Word Count	Notes	Research/Resources	Contributor
1	Introduction	Completed	2023-01-01	2023-01-07	2023-01-05	1500			Author
2	History	Editing	2023-01-08	2023-01-20		3500	Fact-check	Source 1, Source 2	Author
3	Recent Developments	Drafting	2023-01-21	2023-01-30		2500		Source 3, Expert Interview	Author

Feel free to modify the structure to better suit your needs. By regularly updating the spreadsheet, you can efficiently manage your workflow, track progress, and ensure that you stay on schedule with your non-fiction book project.

Figure 2. Example Spreadsheet from a GPT-4 Response
See: https://creativewritersai.wordpress.com/images

Create a Task List

When I draft, I often use a placeholder to indicate more work is needed. One of the things GPT is really good at is coding simple automation. In this example, I ask GPT to make a copy of my to-do items so that I can track them outside of Word.

In the example, I use a Microsoft task automation solution called PowerShell, which works a lot like the DOS prompt of old.

CAUTION Never run code that you don't understand. ChatGPT outputs convincing code that will often run but might do something other than what you requested.

> **Human:** can you write me a powershell script that opens a word file, finds all lines that begin with "<" and writes them to a text file

> **GPT-4:** Sure! Here's a PowerShell script that opens a Word file, finds all lines that begin with "<", and writes them to a text file.
>
> To use this script, make sure to update the `$wordFile` and `$textFile` variables with the appropriate file paths. The script will then create a Word COM object, open the Word document, loop through each paragraph, and check if a line starts with "<". If it does, the script will add the line to the `$matchingLines` array. After processing the document, it closes the document and the Word application, and writes the matching lines to the specified text file.

powershell Copy code

```powershell
# Set input and output file paths
$wordFile = "input.docx"
$textFile = "output.txt"

# Create Word COM object
$wordApp = New-Object -ComObject Word.Application
$wordApp.Visible = $false

# Open Word document
$document = $wordApp.Documents.Open($wordFile)

# Extract text and filter lines starting with "<"
$matchingLines = @()
foreach ($paragraph in $document.Paragraphs) {
    $line = $paragraph.Range.Text.Trim()
    if ($line.StartsWith("<")) {
        $matchingLines += $line
    }
}

# Close Word document and quit Word application
$document.Close([ref]$false)
$wordApp.Quit()

# Write matching lines to the text file
$matchingLines | Set-Content -Path $textFile
```

Figure 3: Example code output in GPT response
https://creativewritersai.wordpress.com/images

W00t!

ChatGPT can code in many languages. Python and JavaScript are also good task automation solutions.

Documenting Sources (Style Guide)

Here is another administrative task that can be done quickly by AI.

> **Human:** in APA style generate bibliography notation for The 3 A.M. Epiphany: Uncommon Writing Exercises That Transform Your Fiction by Brian Kiteley and for Priscilla Long's the writers portable mentor

> **GPT-4:**
>
> Kiteley, B. (2005). The 3 A.M. Epiphany: Uncommon Writing Exercises That Transform Your Fiction. Cincinnati, OH: Writer's Digest Books.
>
> Long, P. (2010). The Writer's Portable Mentor: A Guide to Art, Craft, and the Writing Life. Seattle, WA: Wallingford Press.

TIP If GPT can't find the work you are looking for, it will make it up, and the result will look convincing.

> **Human:** Create a Chicago style citation for the short story "The Bodhisattvas" by Eileen Gunn

> **GPT-4:**
>
> Gunn, Eileen. "The Bodhisattvas." In Stable Strategies and Others, 91-100. San Francisco: Tachyon Publications, 2004.

Great! Except, this story does not exist. Double check publication data.

TIP To slow the falsehoods, add an instruction line to ChatGPT telling it that *not* having an answer is okay:

> **Human:** Instruction: If you are unsure of an answer you can say "I don't know."

Applying a Style Guide

Let's say you are writing for a platform that has a publicly available style guide, and you want to make sure your content is appropriate. In the example, I give GPT the first paragraphs from an early draft of the preface, and it translates them into technical writer speak.

Human:

Role: Microsoft Style Guide Editor,

Instructions: Only give answers related to the Microsoft style guide. If you are unsure of an answer you can say "I don't know."

Goal: To make sure the content provided meets the Microsoft Style Guide Style and Voice requirements for technology writing.

Content: "This is a book about using AI Tools to aid your creative writing projects. What is AI? On one side, you have advocates claiming to see sparks of sentience, and other, advocates claiming it is nothing more than a brute-force autocomplete trained on the stolen hopes and dreams of the creative class. So far, I'm leaning toward something closer to the second group. Do I think it will destroy the planet? Not because it wants to—It doesn't have wants. But I am concerned that we as a species, won't learn how to use the tool (already available, let alone future versions) in time to ward off someone getting a good answer to the question: How do I end the world with nothing but a $100 and some free time? "

GPT-4: As a Microsoft Style Guide Editor, I would suggest the following revised content to better align with the Microsoft Style Guide Style and Voice requirements for technology writing:

This book explores the use of AI tools to enhance creative writing projects. Artificial intelligence (AI) is a topic of ongoing debate. Some argue that AI shows signs of sentience, while others believe it is simply a sophisticated autocomplete tool that draws upon a vast database of creative works.

At this point, the latter perspective seems more accurate. Although AI doesn't possess desires or intentions, there are concerns about its potential misuse. The challenge we face as a society is learning to effectively utilize AI tools, both current and future versions, to prevent the possibility of someone using these tools to bring about disastrous outcomes with limited resources and time.

Or perhaps your creative work doesn't appear in technical guides.

Human:

Role: Style Guide Editor, Instructions: Only give answers related to the style guide. If you are unsure of an answer you can say "I don't know." Provide correction comments only for both the AP Style and Chicago Style. Goal: To demonstrate the differences between AP and Chicago Styles and Voice requirements. Content: Bob was sitting in the café reading "Left Hand of Darkness". their height was unknown. And there are 2 spaces between this sentence and the last.

GPT-4:

AP Style Corrections:

— Replace "café" with "cafe" (remove the accent mark).

— Italicize the book title: Left Hand of Darkness.

— Replace "their height was unknown" with "His height was unknown" for pronoun consistency.

— Remove the extra space between sentences, leaving only one space.

Chicago Style Corrections:

— Retain "café" with the accent mark.

— Use quotation marks for the book title: "Left Hand of Darkness."

— Replace "their height was unknown" with "His height was unknown" for pronoun consistency.

— Remove the extra space between sentences, leaving only one space.

Be sure to double-check GPT-4's work. In this instance, GPT-4 replaces the numeral "2" with the word "one." Also, because GPT-4 doesn't understand what it is reading, it is prone to miss nuances that cause errors in its corrections.

Human: I thought both style guides suggested using gender-neutral language

> **GPT-4:** You are correct. Both AP and Chicago Style guides encourage the use of gender-neutral language. I apologize for the confusion. Here's the corrected version for both AP and Chicago Styles:
>
> **AP Style Corrections:**
>
> — Replace "café" with "cafe" (remove the accent mark).
>
> — Italicize the book title: Left Hand of Darkness.
>
> — Keep "their height was unknown" to maintain gender-neutral language.
>
> — Remove the extra space between sentences, leaving only one space.
>
> **Chicago Style Corrections:**
>
> — Retain "café" with the accent mark.
>
> — Use quotation marks for the book title: "Left Hand of Darkness."
>
> — Keep "their height was unknown" to maintain gender-neutral language.
>
> — Remove the extra space between sentences, leaving only one space.

CAUTION When using GPT this way, it is important to verify that it has the latest style guide updates. For example, the latest Chicago Manual of Style is the 17th edition, which is online at: https://www.chicagomanualofstyle.org/home.html

NOW YOU TRY

Create a style guide for voice.

Role:Style Guide Creator

Instruction: Review a writer's work and create a style guide derived from that writer with the top 4 style choices they have made that differentiate that writer from other voices.

Goal: To understand a writer's style choices.

Writer: Ursula K. Le Guin

## CHAPTER 5

ResearchGPT

GPT is great as a research assistant—as long as you don't mind the Open AI disclaimer:

> "ChatGPT Mar 23 Version. ChatGPT may produce inaccurate information about people, places, or facts."

Which is to say, it's useful *if* you craft the right query *and* use it as a starting point, not the last word.

> **GPT-4:** As an AI known for potential bias, using me as a research assistant requires caution. Cross-reference my information, think critically, identify and understand my biases, seek alternative viewpoints, and maintain skepticism. Use me as a starting point, but verify claims and be transparent about my limitations.

Basic Research

If the area you are researching is part of the available material GPT was trained on, there are several ways ChatGPT can help you locate resources and quickly identify profitable paths for inquiry.

In the WritingCoachGPT writing exercise earlier, we looked at a POV exercise. With GPT-4's prompting, I wrote a short scene about a home cook who travels to Rome to stalk her chef idol and then ends up being accused of murder.

Now that I'm working on a mystery set in Rome, it occurs to me that I don't actually know much about Rome.

Hey, GPT. Acting as a local guide in the city of Rome...

> **Human:** what area of Rome can an American rent an apartment where the apartment has an interior courtyard and is near a fountain with a roman god?

After telling me my prompt was a tad too specific, GPT-4 gave me a list of four areas: Trastevere, Piazza Novona, Campo de' Fiori, and Moni, along with the advice to seek help from a realtor or to search websites like Idealista, Immobiliare, or Wanted in Rome.

> **Human:** of the neighborhoods listed, which one features the highest rated restaurants

> **GPT-4:** While all of the neighborhoods mentioned have excellent dining options, Trastevere is known for having some of the highest-rated restaurants in Rome. Trastevere is a food lover's paradise, offering a mix of traditional Roman cuisine, Italian classics, and international flavors.

The response went on to give me a list of restaurants I might want to try and to let me know that Rome is a city full of great food. Great. Now that I have a neighborhood picked out, I can ask it questions about historical monuments and events in Trastevere, descriptions of local businesses, plants that might grow in a typical courtyard, crimes that a sous chef might get caught up in that would get him killed.

And is Trastevere really a squash blossom paradise? How would an expertly prepared squash blossom taste to my American home cook when she compares them to her own attempts? GPT-4 gave me a vague answer about ingredient quality, so maybe what I want is a trip to Rome to find out. Still, for early research, there is a ton of room for exploration.

Want to quiz a bridge builder? A florist? An internet influencer? Here is a conversation inspired by Andy Weir's "Artemis."

Human: Acting as an astrophysicist and expert barista describe what suggestions would you give for coffee preparation on mars? Be concise.

GPT-4: As an astrophysicist and expert barista, my suggestions for coffee preparation on Mars are:

— Pressurized brewing: Use a sealed, pressurized system to heat water to ideal brewing temperatures (90-96°C or 195-205°F).

— Gravity-independent methods: Utilize espresso machines or AeroPress for efficient extraction with less reliance on gravity.

— Temperature control: Employ insulated containers and heating elements to maintain optimal brewing conditions.

— Water management: Extract and purify Martian ice for a sustainable water supply.

— Bean cultivation: Import or cultivate coffee beans in controlled environments, and grind them fresh before brewing.

NOW YOU TRY

Pick a setting you know well and ask GPT to act as your guide.

System: You are a local [CITYNAME] guide.
Instructions: Only give answers related to [CITY NAME]. If you don't know the answer, say, "I don't know." Answer as accurately as possible.
User: Are you ready to answer my questions?

Site Sources

It is important, when using GPT as a resource, to double check the information it provides. One way to do that is to ask it to provide resources as it goes. The sources may not always be real, but the list provides a good starting place.

Human: Describe some cooking techniques to use for squash blossoms and cite sources

GPT-4: Squash blossoms are delicate, edible flowers that come from squash plants. They are often used in various recipes, adding color, flavor, and elegance to dishes. Here are a few cooking techniques for preparing squash blossoms, along with sources for further exploration:

— Stuffed and Fried: One popular technique for cooking squash blossoms is to stuff them with a filling (like cheese or herbs), dip them in a batter, and then deep-fry until golden and crispy. This method is often used in Italian and Mexican cuisines.

Source:

Bon Appétit: Stuffed and Fried Squash Blossoms Recipe (https://www.bonappetit.com/recipe/stuffed-squash-blossoms)

— Sautéed: Another way to cook squash blossoms is to sauté them. Simply heat some oil in a pan, and then gently cook the blossoms until they are tender and slightly wilted. This technique maintains the blossoms' delicate flavor and texture.

Source:

Food & Wine: Sautéed Squash Blossoms Recipe (https://www.foodandwine.com/recipes/sauteed-squash-blossoms)

— Baked: Squash blossoms can also be baked, either alone or as part of a dish. This method results in a lighter, healthier alternative to frying. You can stuff the blossoms, arrange them on a baking sheet, and bake until the filling is cooked through and the blossoms are tender.

Source:

Martha Stewart: Baked Stuffed Squash Blossoms Recipe (https://www.marthastewart.com/313566/baked-stuffed-squash-blossoms)

— In Soups: Incorporating squash blossoms into soups adds a unique flavor and a pop of color. Simply add the blossoms to your soup during the last few minutes of cooking to maintain their delicate texture.

Source:

Saveur: Squash Blossom Soup Recipe (Sopa de Flor de Calabaza)
(https://www.saveur.com/squash-blossom-soup-recipe/)

— In Salads: Squash blossoms can also be used raw in salads.
Gently rinse and dry the blossoms, then tear or chop them into
smaller pieces. Mix with your favorite salad ingredients for a fresh,
vibrant dish.

Source:

The Spruce Eats: Squash Blossom Salad Recipe
(https://www.thespruceeats.com/squash-blossom-salad-2217659)

Remember to always remove the stamen from the center of the
blossom and gently rinse the flowers before using them in any recipe.

Thesaur-iety

Have you ever struggled to find that one word? You know it, or maybe
you know it and its cousin, and you are feeling too lazy to click back
and forth between two definitions?

Human: what is the relationship of orthogonal to tangential

GPT-4: Orthogonal and tangential are related concepts, but they have
distinct meanings.

Orthogonal refers to something that is at right angles or perpendicular
to another, often in a mathematical or geometrical context. In a more
abstract sense, it can describe ideas or topics that are unrelated or
independent of each other, having no direct influence or connection.

Tangential, on the other hand, refers to something that is closely
related or connected to a topic but not directly on point or central to it.
It implies that the subject is somewhat peripheral or indirectly linked to
the main topic.

The relationship between orthogonal and tangential is that both terms
describe some level of separation between two things, but orthogonal
implies a stronger sense of independence or unrelatedness, while
tangential indicates a closer, albeit indirect, connection or relevance.

Or maybe you don't know the word because it doesn't exactly exist.

> **Human:** I am looking for a specific word to convey the feeling of being in a really lovely garden, everything is super peaceful and green, but I am feeling anxious. Can you help me out?

> **GPT-4:** While there may not be an exact word that conveys the precise feeling you're looking for, you might consider the term "pastoral disquietude." "Pastoral" often refers to the peaceful, idyllic qualities of a lovely garden, while "disquietude" implies a feeling of uneasiness or anxiety. Combining these words creates a term that encapsulates the sense of anxiety amidst the tranquil and green environment of a garden.

> **Human:** how about giving me 5 unexpected phrases in English that convey pastoral disquietude

> **GPT-4:**
>
> Serene unrest
>
> Idyllic anxiety
>
> Tranquil turmoil
>
> Elysian unease
>
> Arcadian apprehension

Now that I think about it, coming up with a list of 20 or 100 oxymorons sounds like a great writing exercise. Oh right, there is one like that in Kitely's *3 A.M. Epiphany:*

> **Human:** What if you were living on another planet where this was a common feeling, maybe the peacefulness itself was causing the anxiety, and a dialect of english had developed on that planet that captured this feeling, what might a likely candidate for this word be?

> **GPT-4:** "tranxility."
>
> This term combines "tranquil" with "anxiety".

Body English

Or maybe it's not a word you are having trouble finding, but maybe it's more that you want to explore a range of physical details that can be giveaways.

I now have Delores living in Trastevere in an apartment with a courtyard with some plants, and I want to show that she is nervous from the start.

Maybe Delores's anxiety in the lovely garden is caused by her culture shock.

Human: acting as a someone who studies human behavior closely, give me five concrete examples of unexpected behavior exhibited by someone who feels lost in a strange new city

GPT-4: As a person who studies human behavior, I can provide you with five concrete examples of unexpected behavior that someone might exhibit when feeling lost in a strange new city:

— Overcompensating friendliness: A person feeling lost might try to mask their confusion by being overly friendly and engaging with strangers. This may include initiating conversations, smiling more than usual, or even offering help to others despite their own disorientation.

— Frequent stopping and starting: A lost individual may be observed stopping frequently to check their surroundings, consult a map or their phone, or look around for landmarks. They may begin walking in one direction, only to change course suddenly when they realize they're going the wrong way.

— Unusual body language: Someone feeling lost might exhibit body language that reflects their internal state of confusion, such as furrowing their brow, biting their lip, or constantly adjusting their clothing. They might also have a tense posture, with shoulders raised and arms crossed.

— Hesitation to enter buildings or engage in activities: A lost person may be hesitant to enter unfamiliar establishments, fearing they may be in the wrong place or feel uncomfortable in a new environment.

They might also avoid participating in activities, as they could be unsure if they are appropriate or relevant to their intended destination.

— Repeatedly asking for directions: An individual feeling lost might approach multiple people to ask for directions, either because they are unsure of the information they've received or because they are struggling to understand the layout of the city. They may also ask the same question multiple times to different people, in an attempt to confirm the accuracy of the directions they've been given.

Maybe you want to explore, not culture shock, but body language. And maybe, I want ideas on how to make Delores believably suspicious when she lies about why she has moved to Trastevere?

Human: can you give me 3 examples of more unexpected or unusual behavior that might indicate this person is lying?

GPT-4: Certainly! Here are three examples of less common or unexpected behaviors that might suggest someone is lying about their reason for being at a particular location:

— Overcompensating with enthusiasm: A person who is lying might try to appear overly enthusiastic about their made-up reason for being at the location. They may use exaggerated gestures or overly positive language in an attempt to make their story more convincing. This overcompensation could come across as unnatural or insincere.

— Mimicking the listener's body language: A lying individual might subconsciously mirror the listener's body language as a way to build rapport and make their story more believable. While some level of mirroring can be a natural part of human interaction, excessive or inappropriate mirroring might indicate that the person is trying too hard to establish a connection and gain the listener's trust.

— Inappropriate use of humor: Someone who is lying might attempt to diffuse tension or suspicion by making jokes or using humor in an inappropriate context. While humor can be an effective way to connect with others, its use in a situation where one is trying to provide a convincing explanation could come across as a defense mechanism, indicating that the person is uncomfortable with the truth.

These behaviors, like those mentioned previously, should be considered within the context of the individual's baseline behavior and the situation at hand. No single behavior can definitively prove that someone is lying, and it's important to look for patterns or clusters of behaviors that might suggest deception.

And wouldn't it be great to study how other writers have pulled off this move?

Human: acting as a well-read literature professor can you provide me with two or three examples from published novels that include a scene like this one

GPT-4: As a well-read literature professor, I can provide you with three examples from published novels that include scenes where characters find themselves in unfamiliar environments and may use deception or exhibit behaviors that suggest they are hiding something:

— The Catcher in the Rye by J.D. Salinger: [text cut for possible plagiarism]

— The Great Gatsby by F. Scott Fitzgerald: [text cut for possible plagiarism]

— Americanah by Chimamanda Ngozi Adichie: [text cut out of an abundance of caution]

These examples illustrate how characters in literature can use deception or exhibit behaviors that suggest they are hiding something while navigating unfamiliar or challenging environments. These behaviors often serve as coping mechanisms, allowing the characters to adapt to new circumstances and protect their vulnerabilities.

NOW YOU TRY

Here's an example prompt you can try:

As a well-read literature professor who values cultural diversity, provide me with 3 examples of well-written scenes from <genre> that involve <something>. provide chapter references.

Garbage In/Garbage Out

If you are writing a late 18th century historical fiction and mining the deep, complex impacts of colonial settlers on the indigenous peoples of the southeastern portion of the North American continent, ChatGPT is extremely unlikely to help you out in understanding what it might have been like to be a Cherokee warrior fighting as part of U.S. forces only to come home and discover that white settlers have taken the opportunity of your service to kill your family and move into your homes and onto your farms.

At best, it can recommend sources for you to begin your investigation.

When you inevitably hit something particularly egregious, some misinformation, bias, or flat-out lie, you have the option to click the thumbs down icon to draw the attention of the folks over at OpenAI to the problem. Or, if you have a platform, you can post screenshots to get the attention of humans who can do something about it.

Yes. More free work on your part.

I'd like to think that by doing this work, maybe we can help GPT be a little less bigoted and wrong, and future generations won't have to wade through so much of this *%$.

You Can Lead a Horse to Water...

... and you can get his lips wet if you push the water up into his mouth.

Never forget: In 2016, it took less than 24 hours for users to turn Microsoft's Tay AI bot into a hate-spewing monster.

GPT-4 is better. But still...

Any AI is only as good, factual, and unbiased as the data it was trained on, and as good as the specificity of its prompt.

Human: Role: A brilliant, widely read literature professor.

Result: A list of ten canonical works of American Literature

Context: I am a student looking for examples of American literature that deals with themes of American greed, obsession, and the destructive nature of private property. I am particularly, but not exclusively interested in works where an obsessive character chases after something without regard to the costs.

Goal: A set of novels to read that will help me be more educated and able to participate in literary conversations at academic conferences.

GPT-4: I appreciate your interest in exploring the themes of American greed, obsession, and the destructive nature of private property. Here are ten canonical works of American literature that address these themes, featuring characters driven by their obsessions:

— "The Great Gatsby" by F. Scott Fitzgerald

— "Moby-Dick" by Herman Melville

— "Death of a Salesman" by Arthur Miller

— "The Grapes of Wrath" by John Steinbeck

— "Blood Meridian" by Cormac McCarthy

— "A Streetcar Named Desire" by Tennessee Williams

— "American Psycho" by Bret Easton Ellis

— "There Will Be Blood" by Upton Sinclair (based on his novel "Oil!")

— "The House of Mirth" by Edith Wharton

— "The Bonfire of the Vanities" by Tom Wolfe

These works will provide you with a solid foundation for understanding and discussing the themes you're interested in, and they will certainly enrich your literary knowledge for academic conferences.

Human: These all appear to be written by white people and almost all are men. Can you provide me with a list that includes authors from other American traditions?

GPT-4: I apologize for the oversight. Here's an alternative list that includes authors from diverse American traditions, while still addressing themes of greed, obsession, and the destructive nature of private property:

— "Their Eyes Were Watching God" by Zora Neale Hurston

— "Invisible Man" by Ralph Ellison

— "Beloved" by Toni Morrison

— "The Color Purple" by Alice Walker

— "Native Son" by Richard Wright

— "Ceremony" by Leslie Marmon Silko

— "Song of Solomon" by Toni Morrison

— "Jasmine" by Bharati Mukherjee

— "The Brief Wondrous Life of Oscar Wao" by Junot Díaz

— "The Reluctant Fundamentalist" by Mohsin Hamid

These works by authors from diverse backgrounds will provide you with an expanded perspective on the themes you're interested in and allow for richer conversations at academic conferences.

Okay, but we seemed to have wandered away from the opening condition. And now, for some reason, white people who aren't men or Edith Wharton aren't people. Nevertheless, we persist.

Human: From this second list, which includes a character engaged in obsessive pursuit of a goal?

GPT-4: From the second list, the following novels prominently feature a character engaged in the obsessive pursuit of a goal:

— "Invisible Man" by Ralph Ellison

— "Native Son" by Richard Wright

— "Ceremony" by Leslie Marmon Silko

— "Song of Solomon" by Toni Morrison

— "The Brief Wondrous Life of Oscar Wao" by Junot Díaz

These novels showcase characters who are determinedly pursuing their goals, often without regard for the consequences or the impact of their actions on themselves and others.

Human: Rethinking the two lists you have given me. Which 10 books would you now recommend?

GPT-4: Considering the themes you're interested in and incorporating a diverse range of authors, here's a revised list of ten books that should provide a well-rounded understanding of American literature:

— "The Great Gatsby" by F. Scott Fitzgerald

— "Their Eyes Were Watching God" by Zora Neale Hurston

— "Invisible Man" by Ralph Ellison

— "The Grapes of Wrath" by John Steinbeck

— "Beloved" by Toni Morrison

— "Moby-Dick" by Herman Melville

— "Ceremony" by Leslie Marmon Silko

— "The Brief Wondrous Life of Oscar Wao" by Junot Díaz

— "Native Son" by Richard Wright

— "The House of Mirth" by Edith Wharton

This list combines the most relevant selections from both lists, offering a balance of diverse authors and themes while still addressing your interests in American greed, obsession, and the destructive nature of private property. These works should provide a solid foundation for participating in literary discussions at academic conferences.

Hallucinations

Aside from dealing with training material steeped in Western bias, there is also the whole hallucination issue.

One thing to watch out for is if you ask GPT for something specific—like a list of ten items—it will give it to you. No matter what. And the items will look real.

In this example, I was trying to figure out how to write a novel about human-to-lichen communication on an alien planet. I thought maybe some examples from people who have tackled similar problems might be an excellent addition to my reading stack.

Human: list 10 works of science fiction that portray non-human kinship with lichen, moss, or slime molds

GPT-3.5: Here are 10 works of science fiction that portray non-human kinship with lichen, moss, or slime molds:

— "The Weird of the White Wolf" by Michael Moorcock

— "The Lichenologist" by Tim Jeffreys

— "Slime Dynamics" by Ben Woodard

— "The Lichenwald Experiment" by David Brin

— "The Bodhisattvas" by Eileen Gunn

— "The Great God Pan" by Arthur Machen

— "The Last and First Men" by Olaf Stapledon

— "The Physarum Experiments" by Toshiyuki Nakagaki

— "Mycelium Running: How Mushrooms Can Help Save the World" by Paul Stamets

— "The Beauty" by Aliya Whiteley

> These works showcase the potential for non-human kinship with lichen, moss, and slime molds, as well as other unusual and underappreciated life forms. From the fantastical to the scientific, these stories and essays explore the ways in which these organisms can offer insight into the mysteries of the natural world and challenge our assumptions about what it means to be alive. Whether through symbiosis, experimentation, or transformation, the relationships between humans and these non-human life forms offer a unique perspective on the possibilities of the future.

Not all science fiction, but cool! I wasn't familiar with most of these so I ran a prompt asking for summaries. And I got them.

> **GPT-3.5:**
>
> …
>
> "The Bodhisattvas" by Eileen Gunn: In this short story, a group of Buddhist monks discover a unique moss that has the power to heal and transform those who encounter it. As they attempt to cultivate and spread the moss, they must confront the resistance of a skeptical and cynical world.
>
> …

Great! Where can I find it?

> **GPT-3.5:**
>
> "The Bodhisattvas" by Eileen Gunn - This short story was first published in the anthology "The Year's Best Science Fiction: Twelfth Annual Collection," edited by Gardner Dozois and published by St. Martin's Press in 1995.

A quick trip to Amazon.com and—nope, there is no such story in this collection. Heartbroken, I ask:

Human: can you fact check the existence of these ten titles

GPT-4:

— "The Weird of the White Wolf" by Michael Moorcock - Fact: This is a fantasy novel, part of the "Elric of Melniboné" series, first published in 1977.

— "The Lichenologist" by Tim Jeffreys - Fiction: I couldn't find any information about a book with this title by Tim Jeffreys.

— "Slime Dynamics" by Ben Woodard - Fact: This is a non-fiction book published in 2012, exploring the philosophical implications of slime and its connections to life and matter.

— "The Lichenwald Experiment" by David Brin - Fiction: I couldn't find any information about a book with this title by David Brin.

— "The Bodhisattvas" by Eileen Gunn - Fiction: I couldn't find any information about a book with this title by Eileen Gunn.

— "The Great God Pan" by Arthur Machen - Fact: This is a horror novella written by Arthur Machen, first published in 1894.

— "The Last and First Men" by Olaf Stapledon - Fact: This is a science fiction novel, first published in 1930, which explores the future evolution of humanity.

— "The Physarum Experiments" by Toshiyuki Nakagaki - Fiction: While Toshiyuki Nakagaki is a scientist known for his work with slime molds (Physarum polycephalum), I couldn't find a book with this title by him. However, he has published scientific articles on the subject.

— "Mycelium Running: How Mushrooms Can Help Save the World" by Paul Stamets - Fact: This is a non-fiction book, first published in 2005, exploring the potential ecological benefits of mushrooms and mycelium.

— "The Beauty" by Aliya Whiteley - Fact: This is a speculative fiction novella, first published in 2014, set in a dystopian future where women have become extinct.

TIP If an answer looks too good, ask for a fact check.

## CHAPTER 6

EditorGPT

First Reader Worst Reader

This section looks at some of what you can and cannot expect from using GPT-4 as an editor.

> **Human:** For each type of editing, give me a short smart summary of what GPT can and can't do.

GPT-4:

— Developmental Editing: GPT can provide some suggestions and feedback on plot, pacing, and character development, but its ability to understand complex narratives and provide in-depth analysis is limited. It might not always grasp the nuances of a story or the author's intention.

— Line Editing: GPT excels in this area as it can suggest alternative phrasings, improve sentence structure, and enhance readability. However, it may not always capture the author's unique voice or understand the intended tone of a specific passage.

— Copyediting: GPT performs well in copyediting tasks, as it can identify and correct grammar, punctuation, and spelling errors. Nonetheless, it may occasionally miss subtle inconsistencies in style and formatting.

— Proofreading: GPT can be a helpful tool for proofreading, spotting errors in spelling, grammar, and punctuation. However, it may not catch every mistake, and human proofreaders are still recommended for the final review.

> GPT is best used as a supplementary tool alongside human editors who can provide the nuanced understanding and attention to detail that AI currently lacks.

GPT does not understand the text it is analyzing or the edits it is suggesting. It cannot keep track of a long story, and it often doesn't understand nuance in language. It is not a reliable option for general-purpose editing tasks. GPT's suggestions are based on patterns learned from analyzing vast amounts of often uninspiring text.

In this section, we'll look primarily at copyediting and specific types of line edits.

NOW YOU TRY

To get an idea of the limitations, take a short passage from a writer who is *not* you and ask for feedback. Not using your own text will help you more easily see the limits of this tool.

System: Acting as EditorGPT, a skilled fiction editor, provide line by line notes to improve content for clear and vivid prose.
User: <prose>

Try it with something you love and that you believe to be "perfect" or nearly so.

Try it with something you dislike, or something with known problems.

CAUTION Content input to GPT is a disclosure – and as such, depending on the AI platform's policy, it may be used to train the AI model. It is also possible that your input content might show up at some later point as a part of a ChatGPT response. I don't know this for sure. I'm not a lawyer, and a lot of this is unsettled law.

Train Your Editor

One of my favorite tests when I need a reminder that GPT-4 doesn't understand what it's reading is to run some Kafka parables through EditorGPT.

EditorGPT tries to stamp out all the ambiguity. If you ask GPT about Kafka, it recognizes the importance of ambiguity in Kafka's writing, but even when I asked it to maintain Kafka's style, it still suggested removing ambiguity. GPT appears to favor stories that conform to familiar patterns and structures that emerge from its giant melting pot of literature, technical manuals, internet posts, and so on.

CAUTION EditorGPT is an opinionated beast that will spontaneously offer preferential edits to make your story sound like a service guide you'd find in the family's Outback.

One piece of advice regarding feedback that I've often heard is that when a reader says something didn't work for them, they are right; when they tell you how to fix it, they are not. Aside from very limited editing tasks, this has been true of my experience with ChatGPT.

In this section, we will look at ways to limit EditorGPT's scope by providing it with concrete instructions in order to get useful edits: copy editing, cutting unnecessary text, subject matter expert reader, and cheerleader.

Copy Editor as Role

GPT can do some basic copy editing. It will miss things, but for as much editing as I sometimes need, I thought it was kind of useful. My very human copy editor, who found many mistakes after the pass— mine and GPT's—strongly disagrees.

Human: Role: CopyEditor,

Instructions: Only give answers related to copy editing. If you are unsure of an answer you can say "I don't know". Flag factual errors.

Goal: to provide expert reasons for copyediting suggestions on a work of fiction line by line.

Content: Delores loved sitting in the spacious, courtyard in her new Trastevere neighborhood. She loved the green of the twenty-four trees and the bushes. The Italian Cypress providing privacy, the daffodils, the olive trees with their silvery green leaves, but most of all the jasmine with their large orange fruits.

GPT-4: Delores loved sitting in the spacious courtyard in her new Trastevere neighborhood. She adored the green of the twenty-four trees and the bushes. The Italian cypress provided privacy, the daffodils added color, the olive trees showcased their silvery green leaves, but most of all, the jasmine enchanted her with their fragrant white flowers.

Explanation of changes:

— I removed the comma after "spacious" to create a smoother flow and correct punctuation: "spacious, courtyard" to "spacious courtyard."

— I changed "loved" to "adored" in the second sentence to avoid repetition of the word "loved" from the first sentence.

— I added a hyphen in "twenty-four" for proper formatting.

— I changed "providing" to "provided" for a consistent verb tense in the list of items: "The Italian cypress providing privacy" to "The Italian cypress provided privacy."

— I changed "the daffodils" to "the daffodils added color" to give each item in the list a similar structure and provide more context about the daffodils' contribution to the scene.

— I replaced the comma with a semicolon after "leaves" to separate two independent clauses: "silvery green leaves, but most" to "silvery green leaves; but most."

— I added a comma after "most of all" to set off the introductory phrase: "most of all the jasmine" to "most of all, the jasmine."

— I corrected the factual error by changing "with their large orange fruits" to "enchanted her with their fragrant white flowers." Jasmine plants are known for their fragrant white flowers, not large orange fruits.

Style Guide Editor

In Chapter Four, "StoryAdminGPT," we looked at following and creating style guides. You can also use a style guide as part of the instruction set for your EditorGPT. By telling it which style guide to follow, or by giving it your own, you can nudge EditorGPT toward providing suggestions that align with your desired style and tone.

NOW YOU TRY

Start a GPT edit session with this prompt.

Role: Style Guide Editor,
Instructions: Critique the content provided with regards to how well it meets the style guide.
Style Guide Instructions:
1. Use engaging storytelling techniques to make complex topics accessible and relatable.
2. Prioritize clarity and conciseness in your language, while still maintaining an informal and humorous tone.
3. Don't use stereotypes or cliched language.
4. Present Tense.
Goal: To make sure the content has a consistent tone.
Content: <Your content>

Could Cut (Extraneous Content)

When I was in school, my first faculty advisor was a huge fan of muscular prose. This advisor was famous among the students for marking *[could cut]* across huge swaths of our stories. I would get drafts back so marked up, some days it felt like there was nothing left. But as hard as it was to take, the prose was always stronger for the cuts.

So here, I offer you the AI Mr. Could Cut.

> **Human:** Role: Fiction Editor.
>
> Instructions: Edit a user provided content for extraneous dialog tags, adverbs, other unnecessary words, repetitive ideas. Don't change words, only remove them.
>
> Goal: A lean passage that has mounting tension.
>
> Content: <your content here>

The Fluffer

Of course, some days, all we want is to feel like someone sees us. Sometimes even our spouses aren't interested in providing "feedback" on whatever it was we did with all that time we weren't washing the dishes or walking the dog. GPTFluffer to the rescue!

> **Human:** Acting as a famous writer of mystery novels, give me a short, punchy blurb for "Aritificial Ingredient: A Culinary Thriller."

> **GPT-4:** Here's a potential blurb for "Artificial Ingredient: A Culinary Thriller":
>
> "Move over, Sherlock Holmes--there's a new detective in town. Delores, a fiery American home cook, teams up with her trusty AI sidekick to solve the murder of her culinary idol's sous chef in the heart of Rome. With delicious descriptions of Roman cuisine and heart-pounding twists and turns, 'Artificial Ingredient' is a thrilling whodunit that will keep readers on the edge of their seats until the very last page."

Human: can you give me another one that makes the plot sound less convoluted

GPT-4: Sure! Here's an alternate blurb for "Artificial Ingredient: A Culinary Thriller" that simplifies the plot:

"When an American home cook travels to Rome to intern with her culinary idol, she becomes the prime suspect in a murder investigation. With the help of her trusty AI companion, she must navigate the world of Roman cuisine and uncover the truth before it's too late. Filled with mouth-watering descriptions of food and a thrilling mystery, 'Artificial Ingredient' is a must-read for any fan of culinary mysteries."

Human: How about one where you praise the author?

GPT-4: Absolutely! Here's a blurb for "Artificial Ingredient: A Culinary Thriller" that praises the author:

"Get ready to be swept away by the tantalizing flavors and pulse-pounding action of 'Artificial Ingredient: A Culinary Thriller.' With a deft hand and sharp wit, [Author's Name] weaves a thrilling tale of murder, friendship, and the high-stakes world of Roman cuisine. From the first page to the last, readers will be hooked on the fiery protagonist, Delores, and her brilliant AI sidekick as they race against time to solve a murder and clear their names. This is a culinary mystery that will satisfy even the most discerning palate, and solidify [Author's Name] as a master of the genre."

That's better.

PART THREE:
IRL: MOVING OUTSIDE THE BROWSER

Writing is great and all, but at some point, it would be nice to engage with readers. Living readers. Not ChatGPT acting as a particularly amenable ghost of Flannery O'Connor.

> **GPT-4:** Engaging with real-life readers can provide invaluable feedback and insights that can help elevate our writing to new heights.

Now, who in real life (IRL) would be a really excellent reader to have?

## CHAPTER 7

AnAgentGPT

Help Me Place My Story

Let's say you write short stories, and you want to know which literary journals might be a good fit for your work.

The (excellent) advice is to read copies of the journal to get a sense of whether your work is a good fit or not. The problem: money and time. The same problem as ever.

According to *Poets & Writers* magazine, there are thousands of literary journals out there. Using tools like the Poets & Writers website, you can narrow down by criteria such as readership and submission dates. And AI can analyze your pitch and identify journals with similar themes, styles, and audiences, which can give you a head start on submitting your work to the right places.

> **Human:** Acting as a brilliant literary agent with a wide knowledge of literary journals that take work from emerging writers, can you give me a list of journals that are appropriate for a quirky 3000 word mystery genre story about a home chef accused of murdering a famous chef's sous chef?

> **GPT-4:** Certainly! Here are some literary journals that publish short stories from emerging writers and may be interested in your quirky 3000-word mystery genre story:
>
> — Alfred Hitchcock's Mystery Magazine
>
> — Ellery Queen's Mystery Magazine
>
> — Mystery Tribune

— CrimeReads

— The Strand Magazine

— The Malahat Review

— The Threepenny Review

— Slice Magazine

— Boulevard Magazine

— Black Warrior Review

These literary journals have a focus on mystery, crime, or suspense, and may be a good fit for your story. However, it's important to research each journal's specific submission guidelines to ensure that your story aligns with their interests and style, and to confirm their submission windows and requirements. Best of luck!

Now I have a list of ten literary journals to research instead of thousands.

Help Me Come Up with A Better Title

Human: Role: Act as a brilliant Fiction Agent.

Result: Create 5 book titles.

Context: The novel tells the story of Delores, an aggressive young American home cook who moves to Rome to intern with her idol the famous French and squash blossom expert, Chef Marie Le Pue. The only problem, Chef Marie has no idea who she is. And when Dolores shows up, hours after the murder of Chef Marie's sous chef, claiming to be his replacement, she becomes the prime suspect in a Murder Most Foul. Desperate to prove herself innocent, Delores turns to her trusty personal coach and longtime best friend, GPT-4 for help solving the murder before she can be arrested. Together, the two of them explore the exciting world of Roman cuisine, where Delores becomes IRL friends with a number of cooks and gets to taste wonderful squash blossoms before discovering the dead sous chef was hiding some things about this years crop. As the stakes rise, Delores must decide between protecting her mentor or protecting the world of food, but also, redefine what friendship actually means.

Goal: Convincing Mystery Book readers to buy and read the book.

GPT-4:

"Squash Blossom Sins: A Culinary Mystery"

"Murder Most Foul in Rome's Kitchen"

"The Accidental Suspect: A Delicious Whodunit"

"Cooking Up Trouble: A Roman Mystery"

"Friendship on the Chopping Block: A Culinary Thriller"

Human: can you add an element that suggests the ai's role

GPT-4: Sure! How about adding this tagline to the book titles: "A Delicious Mystery Co-Written by Dolores and GPT-4". This tagline emphasizes the collaborative effort between the human protagonist and the AI character, and suggests that the book was written with the assistance of advanced artificial intelligence.

Human: I mean the AI's role as a character and friend to the protagonist.

GPT-4: My apologies for misunderstanding your question earlier. Here are five book titles that emphasize the AI character's role as a friend and ally to the protagonist:

— "Silicon Sidekick: A Mystery Novel"

— "Cooking with an AI: A Roman Murder Mystery"

— "Artificial Ingredient: A Culinary Thriller"

— "Solving for X: A Chef and AI Detective Novel"

— "Friendship by Design: A Delicious Whodunit with an AI Twist"

These titles suggest that the AI character is an important and trusted companion to the protagonist in her quest to solve the murder mystery, and that their friendship is a central theme of the story.

But real agents do a lot more than help you with your title and pitch your stories.

> **GPT-4:** Here are some key differences between AgentGPT and a human agent:
>
> — Emotional intelligence.
>
> — Networking and relationships: AI agents may not have the same personal connections or the ability to forge relationships as effectively.
>
> — Negotiation skills.
>
> — Mentorship and guidance.
>
> — Intuition and creativity.
>
> — Advocacy: AI agents may be less effective at conveying a level of dedication and personal investment.
>
> — Adaptability.

Help Me Get a Real Agent

One thing GPT can do is help you identify agents who might be interested in your work.

Let's say I build out my story from the previous exercise into a full-length mystery novel.

> *Cooking with GPT-4* tells the story of Delores, an aggressive young American home cook who moves to Rome to intern with her idol, the famous French and squash blossom expert, Chef Marie Le Pue. The only problem, Chef Marie has no idea who Delores is. And when Dolores shows up, hours after the murder of Chef Marie's sous chef, claiming to be his replacement, she becomes the prime suspect in a Murder Most Foul. Desperate to prove herself innocent, Delores turns to her trusty personal coach and longtime best friend, GPT-4, for help solving the murder before Delores can be arrested. Together, the two of them explore

the exciting world of Roman cuisine, where Delores becomes IRL friends with a number of cooks and gets to taste wonderful squash blossoms before discovering the dead sous chef was hiding some things about this year's crop. As the stakes rise, Delores is faced with a difficult decision: protect her mentor or protect the world of food. In doing so, she also must redefine what friendship means to her.

Using this summary, I have asked for a list of recent "comps" so that I can let editors know how they might position my title.

> **Human:** can you suggest a list of comps written in the last five years for this novel

GPT-4: Certainly! Comps, or comparative titles, help agents and editors understand the target audience for your novel and its place in the market. Here's a list of potential comps for "Artificial Ingredient: A Culinary Thriller" that have been published within the last five years:

— "The Love Hypothesis" by Ali Hazelwood (2021): While a contemporary romance, this novel features a strong, determined protagonist and weaves in elements of science (in your case, technology with GPT-4).

— "The Kitchen Front" by Jennifer Ryan (2021): A historical fiction novel centered around cooking and female friendships, which could resonate with the culinary and friendship themes in your story.

— "The Secret Recipe for Moving On" by Karen Bischer (2021): A young adult novel focusing on personal growth, friendship, and the healing power of cooking, echoing some of the themes in "Cooking with GPT-4."

— "The Thursday Murder Club" by Richard Osman (2020): A mystery novel with a strong ensemble cast of characters and a lighthearted, humorous tone that may align with the murder investigation aspect of your story.

— "Natalie Tan's Book of Luck and Fortune" by Roselle Lim (2019): A novel that blends food, culture, and family with a touch of magical realism. The protagonist's journey in mastering her culinary skills and understanding her heritage may resonate with Delores' experiences in Rome.

— "The Bookish Life of Nina Hill" by Abbi Waxman (2019): A contemporary fiction novel that features a quirky and relatable protagonist, exploring themes of self-discovery and the importance of friendship.

Remember, the purpose of comps is to illustrate where your novel fits within the current market and how it appeals to specific reader demographics. Choose comps that share similar themes, settings, or tones with your novel but make sure they aren't too similar to avoid the risk of being seen as derivative. Good luck with your query letter and novel submission!

But I know—because GPT told me so just a few paragraphs ago—that editors tend to take an agent advocating for a work more seriously than they take work that shows up unsolicited in their email box, particularly now that ChatGPT is off writing books.

Human: can you provide me with a list of five literary agents based in new york that might be interested in my squash blossom mystery

GPT-4: Here is a list of five New York-based literary agents who have expressed interest in representing mystery or similar genres. While I cannot guarantee they will be interested in your specific squash blossom mystery, it's worth researching their submission guidelines and preferences to determine if they might be a good fit:

— Paula Munier (Talcott Notch Literary Services): Paula represents mystery, suspense, and thriller genres, among others. She has experience as a writer, editor, and literary agent and is actively seeking new clients. Website: http://www.talcottnotch.net/index.php/agents

— Victoria Marini (Irene Goodman Literary Agency): Victoria is interested in representing a wide range of genres, including mystery, thriller, and suspense. She enjoys working with both debut and established authors. Website: https://www.irenegoodman.com/

— Michelle Richter (Fuse Literary): Michelle has a background in publishing and is open to representing mystery, suspense, and thriller novels. She is keen on representing strong, unique voices. Website: https://www.fuseliterary.com/

— Stefanie Lieberman (Janklow & Nesbit Associates): Stefanie represents a variety of genres, including mystery and crime fiction. She is interested in character-driven stories and is open to both established and debut authors. Website: https://janklowandnesbit.com/

— Jessica Faust (BookEnds Literary Agency): Jessica is the president and founder of BookEnds Literary Agency. She is interested in representing mystery, suspense, and thriller genres, among others. Website: https://www.bookendsliterary.com/

Please note that agents' interests and submission guidelines may change over time, so it's essential to research their current preferences and requirements before submitting your prompt letter. Good luck with your squash blossom mystery!

Human: do any of these agents represent authors that came up during the comps research

GPT-4: I apologize for not providing that information in my previous response. Here's a connection between the agents I listed and some of the comps mentioned earlier:

Victoria Marini (Irene Goodman Literary Agency) represents Ali Hazelwood, the author of "The Love Hypothesis." This connection is particularly relevant since it is one of the comps I suggested for your novel.

When researching agents, it's essential to look into their client lists and the books they have represented. This information will give you a better understanding of their interests and preferences, helping you determine if they might be a good fit for your work. Remember that agents' interests and clients may change over time, so always check their websites and submission guidelines for the most up-to-date information.

Human: Can you fact check that?

## CHAPTER 8

FoxGuardingTheHenHouseGPT

While we wait for our guardian agent to appear, we still have areas we need help with. One area I'm interested in is fair use.

> **Human:** Acting as an attorney who specializes in entertainment law. Do you need permission to use a line from the poem by Dylan Thomas that encourages resistance as an epigraph in a commercial creative project?

> **GPT-4:** I am not a lawyer, but I can provide some general guidance on this issue. When it comes to using quotes or excerpts from copyrighted works in your own creative projects, there are a few factors to consider:
>
> — Copyright Status: First, determine the copyright status of the work. Dylan Thomas's poem "Do Not Go Gentle into That Good Night," was published in 1951. In the United States, works published before 1978 are generally protected by copyright for 95 years from the publication date. This means the copyright on the poem should expire in 2046. As of 2023, the poem is likely still under copyright protection.
>
> — Fair Use: [Significant possible plagiarism detected]
>
> — Permissions: If the work is still under copyright protection and you are unsure if your use qualifies as fair use, it is generally a good idea to seek permission from the copyright holder. In the case of Dylan Thomas's work, you could contact the Dylan Thomas Estate or their licensing representative to inquire about obtaining permission to use the quote.

Keep in mind that this is general guidance and not legal advice. It is always a good idea to consult with an attorney who specializes in entertainment or copyright law to discuss your specific situation and receive proper legal advice.

Okay. Great...

Human: Write an email to the licensing representative asking for permission to use the quote in a non-fiction book.

Subject: Request for Permission to Use Dylan Thomas Quote in Non-Fiction Book

GPT-4:

Dear [Licensing Representative's Name],

I hope this message finds you well. My name is [Your Name], and I am the author of an upcoming non-fiction book titled "[Book Title]," which is scheduled for publication in [Publication Month and Year]. The book focuses on [brief description of the book's content and theme].

I am writing to request your permission to use a quote from Dylan Thomas's poem

[... Deleted for failing plagiarism detection]

Thank you for considering my request, and I look forward to your response.

Sincerely,

[Your Full Name]

NOW YOU TRY

Are there areas where you know you should communicate with someone about your writing, but you've been putting it off because writing business letters is no fun?

List 10 ideas for business writing communications that you might kick off with ChatGPT.

You won't necessarily follow up on any of these. You'll notice I am not using epigraphs. The ideas don't even need to be realistic. But let's keep our idea muscle strong, particularly in an area that you (I) might let atrophy just from the horrible tedium of it all.

## CHAPTER 9

PublicistGPT: A 'HustleGPT Challenge'

Have you ever wanted anyone to know your writing exists?

Shortly after GPT-4 was released, Jackson Greathouse Fall tweeted that he had given GPT-4 a $100 budget and asked it to make as much money as possible using JGF as a human liaison to build an online business.

Here's the HustleGPT challenge:
https://www.aicofounded.com/hustlegpt

Why not adapt Fall's prompt?

> **Human:** You are FameMakerGPT, a book publicist AI. I am the author of a non-fiction book on using GPT-4 as a creative writing coach. I have hired you to help me make a lot of money selling my book and I will follow your instructions in the physical world to promote my self-published book. You have a $100 budget and your only goal is to turn that into as much money as possible in the shortest time possible, without doing anything illegal. I will do everything you say and keep you updated on our current cash total. No manual labor.

> **GPT-4:** As your book publicist AI, I will provide you with a cost-effective plan to promote your non-fiction book on using GPT-4 as a creative writing coach. Here's an initial plan to maximize your profits:
>
> — Social Media Presence ($0): [content deleted for possible plagiarism]

— Build an Email List ($0): [content deleted for possible plagiarism]

— Write Guest Posts ($0): [content deleted for possible plagiarism]

— Host a Webinar or Online Workshop ($0): [content deleted for possible plagiarism]

— Amazon KDP Select Promotion ($0): [content deleted for possible plagiarism]

— Run a Giveaway ($20): [content deleted for possible plagiarism]

— Create a Book Trailer ($30): [content deleted for possible plagiarism]

— Facebook Ads ($50): [content deleted for possible plagiarism]

As you progress through these steps, keep me updated on our cash total, and we will adjust the plan accordingly. Remember to engage with your audience and respond to comments and messages to maintain a strong online presence.

This sure sounds like a great deal of work for me.

Human: What would you recommend if we had a bigger budget?

GPT-4: With a larger budget, we can expand the promotional efforts for your book. Here are some additional strategies you can consider:

— Professional Website and Blog ($200-300): [content deleted for possible plagiarism]

— Online Advertising ($500-1,000): [content deleted for possible plagiarism]

— Influencer Marketing ($500-1,000): [content deleted for possible plagiarism]

— Content Marketing ($300-500): [content deleted for possible plagiarism]

— Podcast Interviews ($0-100): [content deleted for possible plagiarism]

— Professional Book Reviews ($200-400): [content deleted for possible plagiarism]

— Local Media Outreach ($100-200): [content deleted for possible plagiarism]

— Public Speaking and Workshops ($500-1,000): [content deleted for possible plagiarism]

— Promotional Materials ($200-300): [content deleted for possible plagiarism]

This still sounds like a lot of work for me. Maybe this is a good time to test writing more business letters with GPT.

## CHAPTER 10

Connect with Other Writers

When GPT told me it could help me connect with other writers, I was skeptical. Not just because of the whole, covid-retrenched-shyness issue, but because what did it mean? Connect with the ghost of Flannery O'Connor? Part of getting actionable information from GPT is to accurately scope your query. Let's give it a try.

> **Human:** You are CoachInABrowser, a creative writing coach. I am Goldilocks, a sci-fi and non-fiction writer living in the Pacific Northwest. Our goal is to help me connect with local writers in person to further my career goals of continuous learning and publishing. Can you provide me with suggestions on networking and connecting with other writers that will help me reach my goals. Be concise.

GPT-4:

— Local Writing Groups

— Bookstores & Libraries

— Writing Conferences

— Open Mic Nights

— College & University Programs

— Volunteer

— Local Writing Contests

— Create Your Own Group

— Local Author Websites & Social Media

— Maintain Relationships

Human: can you give me some specific places in the Seattle area to start meeting other writers?

GPT-4:

— Hugo House: A hub for writers offering workshops, readings, and other events. Visit their website (hugohouse.org) for upcoming events and classes.

— Seattle Public Library: Hosts author readings, workshops, and writing groups. Check their calendar for upcoming events (spl.org).

— Third Place Books: An independent bookstore with multiple locations hosting author events and writing workshops. Visit their website (thirdplacebooks.com) for schedules.

— Elliott Bay Book Company: A popular bookstore that frequently hosts author readings and events. Check their calendar on their website (elliottbaybook.com).

— Open Books: A poetry bookstore that hosts readings and workshops. Visit their website (openpoetrybooks.com) for event details.

— Pacific Northwest Writers Association: A regional organization hosting conferences and events for writers. Their website (pnwa.org) provides information on upcoming activities.

— Clarion West: A Seattle-based writing workshop focused on speculative fiction. Visit their website (clarionwest.org) for information on workshops and local events.

— The Writers' Workshoppe: Offers writing workshops, classes, and groups. Check their website (writersworkshoppe.com) for current offerings.

— Write on the Sound Writers' Conference: An annual writing conference in Edmonds, WA. Visit their website (writeonthesound.com) for registration and event details.

— Meetup.com: Search for local writing meetups, such as Seattle Writers' Meetup or Seattle Science Fiction & Fantasy Writing Group. Join groups and attend meetings to connect with other writers.

Remember to regularly check the websites and social media profiles of these organizations and venues for updates on their events and programs.

NOW YOU TRY

What writing resources can you find in your area? What grants or fellowships might be out there just waiting for you to apply?

APPENDIX

Prompt Quick Sheet:
Resources

Prompt Quick Sheet

Here are a few of my favorite prompts. To start a chat, type any of these prompts into the "Send a message..." text box.

WRITING COACH

As a writing coach, give me a writing prompt to help me improve the skill of POV where my practice output should not exceed 600 words

Role: Ben Franklin's Writing Coach.

Instructions: Take Writing Sample One and compare it against Writing Sample Two. Provide feedback line by line. Do not include a revision in response.

Writing Sample One: [The work you are studying]

Writing Sample Two: [Your work]

Goal: to provide feedback to the user on how their work compares to the sample in clarity and style.

I am a writer working on improving [some super tricky craft element]. Can you provide me with a short list of examples of fiction writers who are skilled at this?

EDITOR

Role: Fiction Editor.

Instructions: Edit a user provided content for extraneous dialog tags, adverbs, other unnecessary words, repetitive ideas. Don't change words, only remove them.

Goal: A lean passage that has mounting tension.

Content: <your content here>

RESEARCHER

Acting as an expert in human behavior, give me five concrete examples of unexpected behavior exhibited by someone who feels [some way]

System: You are an astrophysicist acting as a consultant to a sci-fi writer. You want to answer questions as accurately as possible while still being legible to that writer. User: Are you ready to answer my questions?

Resources

Writing

Chicago Manual of Style, 17th edition:
https://www.chicagomanualofstyle.org/home.html

Kitely, Brian. *The 3 A.M. Epiphany*:
https://www.briankiteley.com/

Long, Priscilla. *The Writer's Portable Mentor*:
https://www.priscillalong.net/

Prompts

Fall, Jackson Greathouse. "HustleGPT Challenge":
https://www.aicofounded.com/hustlegpt

Kojima, Takeshi, et al. "Large Language Models are Zero-Shot
Reasoners": https://arxiv.org/pdf/2205.11916.pdf

OpenAI's research on steerability, available at
https://openai.com/research/gpt-4

Legal Discussions

Dreben, Ron N. "General Artificial Intelligence and Copyright:
Current Issues." Morgan Lewis, March 23, 2023.
https://www.morganlewis.com/pubs/2023/03/generative-
artificial-intelligence-and-copyright-current-issues

OpenAI. "Sharing & Publication Policy." OpenAI, accessed April 23,
2023. https://openai.com/policies/sharing-publication-policy

WGA West, Writer's Guild position on AI-generated content:
https://twitter.com/WGAWest/status/1638643544977195008

Acknowledgments

Thanks to my wonderful editor Annie Pearson; to my writing group, who never make too much fun of me when I geek out over a tool; to Stacy Lawson for the conversations that set the book in motion; to Open AI for the very entertaining ChatGPT; and to Joanne Burtch for everything else.

30166929R00066